The Way It Was

A World War II Memoir

By

Jim Hargrove

Master Sergeant, IPW 138, MIS-ETO
Army of the United States
March 14, 1943 to January 18, 1946

ISBN: 0-75961-210-2

This book is printed on acid free paper.

1stBooks - rev. 01/30/01

FOREWORD

In all her long life Mother never threw a letter away, no matter how insignificant it might seem to others. When she died shortly before her 99th birthday, she left countless letters stuck into corners of chests and desks and, sometimes, paper grocery sacks. My efficient nephews, cleaning up the house in preparation for its sale, found the letters and sent me those that I had written to her.

In the sense that I could never have written this account without my own letters to instruct me, sometimes to be quoted verbatim, Mother is my posthumous enabler. I bless her memory for her devotion to me and her reluctance ever to destroy a word written by one she loved.

My second (and happily *inter vivos*) enabler is Marion, my partner of more than 58 years now. She urged me to write this account of my war, using my letters to Mother for documentary recall. The principal purpose of publishing it is to preserve it for our children, who have heard these stories a number of times, for our grandchildren, who have heard them only in part, and for our great-grandchildren still unborn (but not unbidden) who may someday want to know for themselves their great-grandfather's war stories. Perhaps they will be able to feel my loneliness of separation on the one hand, while on the other experiencing the humor, adventure and accomplishment that was also mine.

This is not a hero's story. Neither I nor the great majority of my colleagues in the IPW teams were heroes. As was the case with millions of soldiers, in my service for a cause I was convinced was just I was never in real danger, never endured the kind of discomfort and exhaustion line soldiers endured, and never was called upon to suffer anything worse than loneliness.

This account, then, is simply a story of one soldier's war, sometimes boring, sometimes frustrating, sometimes funny, always looking to a *"Wiederseh'n in der Heimat"* with the ones he loved. It does not undertake to be a universal account of the war for everyone who served in it. It is not a description of each soldier's service. It is only mine, unique to me as each soldier's is unique to himself.

Finally, this is a true story. Its truth is documented by my contemporary letters. It is the truth of what I really did, with all my warts, the truth of an admittedly non-conformist but otherwise morally serious tour of duty. Except where I have used literary license to provide the sense of conversations rather than their exact spoken words, I believe this account to be accurate in all material respects. Infrequently I have added Year 2000 comments to the historical record. Where I have done that, italics have been used to mark the departure from the narrative's calendar.

Jim Hargrove, Senior
Houston, Texas
November, 2000

TABLE OF CONTENTS

Metamorphosis

Jim Hargrove

Camp Beauregard, Louisiana
March 14, 1943

Some months ago I had enlisted in the Army Enlisted Reserve Corps, thus earning myself the time to complete college by going to school year round. Now Mephistopheles had come to claim his part of the bargain. I was invited to present myself for active service in the Army of the United States ("AUS"). The United States Army ("USA") was the designation of the permanent army, a distinction to denote the difference between those of us just in for the duration of the war (plus six months) and those in the regular army.

Marion and Mother brought me from Shreveport to Alexandria and then to the Reception Center at Camp Beauregard (named for Louisiana's most famous military hero of the Civil War). After we had used up all of our time, we acknowledged inevitability and they left without me.

I watched the car slowly exit the gate and start on the 100 mile trip back to Shreveport. It had not been a happy parting – how could it be, when I was entering an unknown situation for an unknown period of time, with unknown consequences? I had no idea where I would be sent from Beauregard; I was here to be dealt out with the others like a pack of cards, some to infantry, some to armor, some to anti-aircraft artillery, some to tank destroyer units, some to "chairborne" jobs. All I knew for sure was that my destiny was not in my own hands (if it ever had been), and that fortune or luck or whatever else would have the principal control over my life until…when? Who could know?

The "reception center" was not intended to be a permanent home and it made no pretense of being one. Standard, bleak barracks, the usual antiseptic but strictly functional latrine, shower and shaving area, a pot-bellied, wood-burning stove in the middle of the sleeping area, at one end a partitioned room for the non-coms stationed there to make the recruits behave. A foot locker at the end of each bed, a brand-new GI duffel bag folded

3

inside, courtesy of the government. No clothes. The uniforms would come later, part of our induction process.

I dumped my few changes of underwear and my extra civilian tennis shirt in the foot locker with my dopp kit. Even though it was half-way through March, it was cold in the barracks and there was a fire going in the pot-belly. I warmed my hands as I watched the poker game occupying one of the nearby beds. I recognized the standard poker game, but I couldn't understand a word of what was being said by the players. I had had three years of college French in addition to two years at Sewanee Military Academy, but this *patois* was beyond me. I appeared to be the lone redneck among a swarm of Cajuns.

Next morning at reveille the appearance of uniqueness was confirmed. The sergeant made a shouting announcement in Cajun, after which most of the recruits took one step forward. A small number, including me, didn't make a move, not knowing what he had said. He switched to English, in which he was perfectly understandable although rather heavily Cajun-accented. "Thank you men for volunteering," he said to the group which hadn't moved. "You will be on KP for the rest of the day after breakfast. Report to the kitchen right after you finish eating."

Welcome to the Army, Private Hargrove!

The next day when the sergeant went through the same routine, I was ready for him. At his command, I stepped forward with the Cajuns. Or so I thought. When I looked around I saw only fellow rednecks. The Cajuns were firmly in place in their original ranks, most with sly smirks on their faces. I knew what was coming: "Report to the kitchen right after breakfast."

I got to know the kitchen personnel pretty well. Most of them were Cajuns. They would probably stay in the reception center kitchen for the whole duration. I developed a skill for making greasy burnt cooking vessels and messy plates clean enough to pass inspection, although I was sure neither Marion nor Mother would have passed me.

And I learned quickly always to put the giant-sized bottles of Tabasco on the tables, no matter what meal it was or what food was on the *menu du jour*.

In between KP, I fitted in the physical and academic examinations and clothing issues and obligatory films of the consequences of VD (venereal diseases) and the other things the Army had prepared to welcome us. My uniforms were a scream: my khaki pants were about six inches too big at the waist and about the same in length, and the shirts looked like tents. I think perhaps the Army was allowing for some shrinkage if we ever got them washed. My boots were so heavy I didn't see how I could make a 20-mile hike in them even without a back pack. And my khaki overseas cap made me look like the original Sad Sack. Fortunately I was already married; I had no need of sharp clothes to attract the opposite sex.

We were supposed to be at the reception center no longer than a week. I was there two weeks, but I must admit that part of the delay might have been my own doing. When I heard the latest rumor, that we were all going to be sent to a West Coast training center to be educated in the ways of war, then to be sent as replacements for our troop casualties on the desert sands of North Africa, I wrote Dad to see if he could ask a friend to tilt me a little toward Camp Wallace and the anti-aircraft business. Also, I put this down as a strong request in my interviews, with some trepidation because I suspected that the Army was just encouraging us to express preferences in order to send us elsewhere. But as others shipped out hither and yon, I began to believe that perhaps I was being saved for the dashing life of an ack-ack gunner even though my eyesight was substantially less than adequate.

You see, I wanted to become an ack-ack man because one did basic training for that at Camp Wallace, Texas, some 40 miles south of Houston toward Galveston. And my wife of some seven months was living with her family in Houston. I had visions of passes every night and week-end furloughs in Houston or Galveston. I had no real love for the 20mm or 40mm anti-aircraft guns that seemed almost never to hit anything anyway. But I did have a real love for the little lady on Harold Street in Houston.

Marion and I first met in the sixth grade of Sydney Lanier Junior High School in Houston. There were four Smith girls in my home room. Three of them were great friends; the fourth was not included in their coterie. She was too quiet and reserved for them. In the eighth grade we began to have dates. I had a date with Evelyn, a delightful young lady who still reminds me (and whoever else is within hearing distance) that she was my first date. Then I had a date with Marion. When I went to Sewanee for high school, we wrote one another and she sent me a picture. When I returned for the summers we had other dates, and by the time Senior High School was over we were "going steady". After a year at Stephens College in Missouri, she transferred to Rice and we went even steadier. After Pearl Harbor we became formally engaged and in August of 1942 we married.

Many of our friends at Rice followed similar paths. Marriage was the vogue then. Of all those marriages, I can think of none that ended in divorce. Fifty-eight years later, only death has been their terminator. Sometimes I wonder why they lasted when so many others, before and after, foundered on the rocks of divorce. Could the war have been a cementing influence?

Imagine my wonderful astonishment when a shipment left Camp Beauregard for Camp Wallace at the end of March, 1943, with me included.

Army life was going to be easy!

Camp Wallace, Texas
April 2, 1943

I had carefully planned how, when our train arrived in Houston for transfer to buses to Camp Wallace, I would fake a heart attack or something like that so I could call Marion at her Mother's and Dad's to tell her of my great good fortune. But when the train emptied it was to march with our duffels on our backs straight into the doors of the bus. There was no chance to call. But it was not much of a long distance charge from Camp Wallace to Houston, and I was sure Marion's Dad wouldn't mind accepting a collect call or two every now and then. I relaxed and enjoyed the warm April air and the smell of the Gulf in the distance.

We were assigned to Battery D of the 32nd A A R T B (Anti-Aircraft Replacement Training Battalion). The next morning after our late arrival at the camp, we began close order drill and the manual of arms with the (obsolete) 1903 Springfield rifle. The cadre corporal was instructing us in the manual of arms. When he gave the command to "port arms", I briskly pulled the rifle up and across my body and grasped it in my left hand with the resounding "smack" that was the way I had learned to do it in the special performance platoon at Sewanee. The corporal was startled and came over to see what kind of an animal I was.

"Have you had previous military experience?" he asked.

"Yes," I replied non-committally. He called the lieutenant over.

"Do 'port arms' again," he ordered. I slapped it hard again. The lieutenant was impressed.

"Where did you learn that?" he asked.

"At Sewanee Military Academy," I replied.

"How long were you there?"

"Three years."

"What was your highest cadet rank?"

"Major," I answered, being careful not to look into his eyes.

7

"Hmmph," he mumbled. Then, "Corporal, have this man teach the manual of arms to another group while you take a second group through close-order drill."

My fellow ack-ack types looked at me with awe. I showed them a few other tricks with the rifle and they almost called me "Sir". I was impressed again with how easy the Army was going to be. What if I had been able to show them a saber drill? They would probably have given me a field commission, I thought.

The next day they transferred me and a few others from Battery D to Battery B. All my show-boating was for naught. I felt like Joseph when the new king arose that knew him not. In Battery B I was just a late-arriving transfer recruit. I would have to start over.

Out drilling the next day, I heard a familiar stentorian baritone voice calling cadence in a group from Battery A, which shared the same drill ground with us. It could be none other than Jess Bessinger, one of my best friends at Rice, who had also been in the ERC but had gone to Fort Sam Houston for his induction to active duty. I waited until we both had a short break and waved at him. He was about as astonished as I was. I found out he and Tommy Sullivan, another friend from Rice, were in my battalion. The prospects for convivial enjoyment of life increased markedly. Jess and I had shared many a Tuesday night of scholarly revelry. Not to mention the solemnly secret sacred handshake of Phi Beta Kappa, into which we had both been initiated at Rice. And all three of us – Tommy Sullivan included – had lady friends living in Houston. I would soon have a car at my disposal so I could run off to Houston every time I had a few minutes of pass-time. Yes, the Army was going to be pretty easy after all.

Basic training was pretty similar no matter what branch of the Army. Learn to drill. Learn to do things with a rifle like shooting it, cleaning it, taking it apart and putting it back together so it worked, and learn what not to do with it, like resting it on the ground barrel-down, or losing it. Learn to tolerate long hikes with heavy packs without fainting. Learn to fix bayonets and look fierce as you jab a straw man set up for your target. Learn to work with the system or, alternatively, how to get around it. Learn to put up with a lot of little "chicken" things the cadre can think up for you. And learn how to get along without passes home.

In anti-aircraft we also had to learn how to work the guns and track on targets, but most of that would come later, after basic training.

For about six weeks I was a model soldier. I did all the little things like policing up the area, taking my turn at KP, mopping up the barracks and the Battery command post; I also did the more meaningful things like learning how to manipulate the anti-aircraft guns, taking long hikes in the broiling Texas Gulf Coast sun, and fighting off the mosquitoes in bivouac in the high swamp grass behind West Beach on Galveston Island.

Along with a lot of others, I had applied for OCS (Officers' Candidate School) as soon as possible after reaching Camp Wallace. We were interviewed once by a low-ranking group, where they asked about our General Classification Test results (I scored 149, comfortably up in the universe of all scores). I was put in line for consideration for Officers' Candidate School at Fort Davis, North Carolina. In June we were notified of our acceptance into OCS and moved to Battalion 28, a special unit for the OCS candidates. I began signing my return address "Candidate" rather than "Private", and felt good about the prospects. Bessinger and Sullivan were also accepted.

Marion began to talk to Nancy Allen Blakemore Renaud, newly married in February, about places to live in North Carolina. Nancy was living close to Fort Bragg. where Fred Renaud was in training with an airborne unit. Things were going well; the Army wasn't so bad, after all.

About the third week of June, without advance intimation of any sort, OCS admissions were closed. No one would be going. It hit us like a brick. We could see ourselves behind the ack-ack guns forever.

We were transferred back from Battalion 28 to our old battalion, but all of us were transferred to Battery A, Bessinger's old battery. All my work with the cadre in Battery B was down the drain again.

The top sergeant of Battery A hated me. When he looked at me his eyes glittered and his fists clenched. I do not remember a single civil word that passed between us – either from him to me or *vice versa*. I don't know why, unless he just didn't like ROTC kids who knew more about the manual of arms than he did. It wasn't because I was a college kid, because Bessinger and Sullivan were from the same class and the same school, and he got along fine with them. But as far as I was concerned he had an antipathy that wouldn't stop. He had saved the command post building as my special province for mopping duties many a night. He didn't think KP could get along without me. And as far as passes were concerned, he might be willing to give me a 2-hour pass on rare occasions, but that was it.

I threw my good soldier image out the window and into the GI garbage can. If that's the way he wanted to play it, I said to myself, I'd show him a few of the other tricks I learned at SMA. In my frequent visits with my mop into his office, usually when everyone had gone home, I searched out the location of the blank books of passes. As I suspected, there were a number of the blank books in the drawer. When I left that night there was one less. To hell with asking him for a pass when I knew the answer before I asked. From now on I would issue my own passes.

It sounds crazy, but really it was a piece of cake. It was a big camp with a lot of people issuing passes. The guards at the gates didn't have any idea who they all were. I had frequently signed passes at SMA where I was Major and Adjutant, running much of the cadet administration. The Commandant of Cadets was a handsome, easy-going gentleman who knew a good job when he saw it. He asked me to handle the issuance of any passes that were to be issued, and to sign his name for him. I practiced his signature until even he had a hard time determining which was which. And just in case I needed a pass for myself or my friends, I took a book of the passes back to my own room.

What did we do with the passes I issued at SMA? First, we made a deal to rent a car from one of the civilian waiters. There were no persnickety items of refueling or insurance coverage or any of the other things one has to resolve before the rented car is turned over to the renter these days. No, a simple transfer of a few dollars to the owner and the car was waiting, with at least a little gas in it. It wasn't fancy or in perfect shape or anything, but it would run. We had no evidence of our right of possession, but we were never stopped or asked for such evidence. It was a smooth operation.

Then a group, usually no more than three or four, would take out for a jaunt to Monteagle down the highway a few miles. There were cafes which stayed open all night in Monteagle, catering mostly to the truck drivers, selling hamburgers and offering juke boxes for a quarter a tune. And beer was sold to anyone with the small change to pay for it. Nobody asked us for IDs, which we didn't have, of course, since nobody had IDs in those days. We had just recently been issued Texas Driver's Licenses for the first time; earlier there were no Driver's Licenses in Texas at all.

One night on such a trip to Monteagle, one of our group had too many beers (I think the number was three!) and was creating a little competition to the juke box. He was a big, solid guy of about 225 pounds from Ohio, one of the mainstays of the line for our football team, and he dwarfed me. He was a good lad if a little slow, and I didn't want him to get in trouble. So I took a deep breath and hit him with what I dearly hoped was my put-to-sleep punch so I could put him in the car and take him home. He shook his head slightly and said, "Jim, you shouldn't have done that."

I knew immediately that he was right. Rather than make the same mistake twice, I summoned up my most persuasive manner and made an attempt to reason with him, that I had just done it for his own good, etc., and that now we really ought to get back to the Academy. He returned to his affable and pacific ways, and with the help of a couple of others, I loaded him into the rented car and we went back to the barracks. The only scary part was climbing up the fire escape ladder to swing around to the window sill on the third floor on our return. Because, you see, it was sleeting with freezing rain, and the ladder was very slick. But no harm was done; we got him back into bed and no one was the wiser.

I was sixteen years old.

With my supply of contraband passes, I went to Houston from Camp Wallace almost every night, a drive of about an hour each way. I stayed with Marion at her Mom's and Dad's house on Harold Street. I left Wallace when the last formation broke up and at the Smiths' I set an alarm which let me make it back to camp in time for reveille in the morning. I arranged for a buddy to answer "Yo" if my name was called at reveille or any unforeseen formation. I never got caught.

...Except one morning the alarm didn't go off. Mrs. Smith came rushing to our room and asked worriedly, "Doesn't Jim have to go back to camp this morning?"

It was 6:30. I leaped up, thinking my good luck had just run out. I grabbed my pass and read it. Sure enough, the pass expired at 6:45, just ahead of the 7:00 a.m. reveille roll call. I hadn't brought along my book of blank passes. What to do, what to do? I would be labeled AWOL, a very bad thing to have on one's record.

Marion's mother offered a suggestion: "I have some white liquid eraser," she said.

"Let's try it," I replied. And we covered the pass expiration time over thickly with the eraser and let it sit while I got dressed. Then I carefully changed the expiration to 9:00 a.m. That ought to give me plenty of time. Of course the pass looked just like what it was – a poorly altered one, obvious to even the most casual inspector. How could I ever expect to get by with that?

But it was all I had. I jumped in the car, pounded the accelerator and set off for Camp Wallace.

"Be sure to let me know what happens," wailed Marion. She could see herself coming to visit me in the stockade.

I drove up to the gate as usual, nodded to the guard and flashed my pass at him. He hardly glanced at it, waving me through quickly to avoid jamming the traffic behind me. I drove over to the parking lot near the barracks and entered by the back door. My friend sidled up to me.

"I answered for you at reveille," he murmured.

"I owe you one," I acknowledged. Then I ran across the street to the Rec Room and used one of the phones on the wall to call Marion to tell her everything was all right. I stayed on the line only about a minute, then ran back to the barracks – and right into the arms (figuratively speaking) of the top sergeant.

"Where the hell have you been?" he asked me none too politely.

"I just had to make a short phone call, Sergeant," I answered.

"You know it's against regulations to visit the Rec Room before 5:30," he pointed out. "That'll cost you three moppings of the office, beginning tonight."

"Great!" I exclaimed with a wide grin. "I'll be there promptly at 6:00 and give it the best cleaning it has ever had."

He looked at me in a puzzled fashion and we went our ways. I laughed for about a half hour and then got back to soldiering. There was no AWOL on my record.

A few days later the OCS group was called to a meeting. We were told that OCS was permanently closed to AA soldiers, but that the Army had a new program that might be even more to our liking. It was something called ASTP – Army Specialized Training Program. We would, if selected, be sent to a participating university and given intensive training in a language for further assignment upon completion of a nine-months' course. We would be selected on the basis of our language aptitude and facility. There would be no advance in grade while at the university, but we would all be given the single stripe of Private First Class, with the corresponding minute increase in pay, effective immediately.

"Captain," I asked when questions were permitted. "Can you tell us a little more about where we might be sent, to help us decide whether to apply for ASTP?"

"There is no application involved in this program," he replied. "The Army will decide whether you will be included. You will go if, when, and where we tell you to go."

"I understand, Captain," I answered. And I did. The Army was in charge again. I might even have to become a model soldier once more.

Texas A & M College
College Station, Texas
July 5, 1943

In July all of our group of former OCS candidates were sent to Texas A & M at College Station, Texas. That didn't sound too bad, although collegiate rivalries between A & M and Rice had been a touchy matter while Bessinger, Sullivan and I were there. We thought we would be there nine months in the program. But we found out quickly that we wouldn't. We would be interviewed and tested again and then dispatched to some other university for the program.

"What languages have you studied in school?" the interviewer inquired.

"French, Spanish, Italian, Portuguese and a couple of weeks of Japanese."

"How much Portuguese?"

"Only one semester. I thought that was all I really needed."

"That's very interesting. Portuguese is a very high priority language."

"It is? I didn't know there was a war there."

"There's not. That's why everyone sends spies there. It's a free-for-all agglomeration of agents from the Axis countries and the Allies," the interviewer offered. "You might enjoy it."

It sounded interesting, all right. It also sounded dangerous. They shoot spies, don't they? But why should I fight it? The Army would send me whithersoever they wished.

15

Jim Hargrove

The University of Wisconsin
Madison, Wisconsin
27 August 1943

    It took the administrators of ASTP some five weeks to decide where to send everyone.

    I had requested permission to travel in private conveyance. Much to my surprise, it was granted, along with a special issue of gas coupons to make the trip to Madison, Wisconsin, home of the University of Wisconsin, which was to be my post for the next nine months. The reason for the private conveyance was easily apprehended: Marion would accompany me, with all her trousseau from our wedding a year ago, which she really hadn't had much opportunity to wear. We would set up housekeeping in some little apartment across from the campus, we said, and I would visit when I could.

    I didn't get my orders until August 23, and I was due to report August 27. This didn't leave us much time to pack and drive the 1200 miles to Madison. We decided to drive straight through without stopping until we reached Chicago, where we would celebrate our first wedding anniversary on August 25. Early the morning of the 24th we left the Smiths' house on Harold Street and drove to Shreveport, where Granny (Mother's mother) was fixing us a fried chicken lunch in Mother's absence from town awaiting the birth of her first grandson.

    After lunch in Shreveport, we drove north through the afternoon and the darkening night, crossing Arkansas and the boot of Missouri, the great Mississippi River and into Centralia, Illinois. There we stopped long enough to have an early breakfast with one of Marion's school friends from her year at Stephens College. I was pretty tired by that time, but surprisingly not sleepy. We continued on to Chicago, interrupted only once by an Illinois highway patrolman who seemed to think we were driving a little fast. When he saw my uniform, the duffel bag and all the suitcases in the back, he

16

waved us on with a warning, which we heeded until he was out of sight.

I had gone to Montrose Elementary School in Houston with a group of kids with whom I had maintained close contact all the way through Rice University. One of them was Bill Mackey, the only one in our class who could solve the arithmetic flash cards faster than I could. He had gone through Meteorology School in the Air Force and was now a Lieutenant stationed in Chicago. When I knew that we were definitely coming to Chicago, I wired him and asked him to get us hotel accommodations for the night of August 25 and to join us in an anniversary party that night – on us. I felt sure he would jump at the chance.

When we reached the outskirts of Chicago I called him to find out which hotel to go to.

"You shouldn't have come through Chicago," he began as soon as he answered the phone. "There's an American Legion convention and there is not a room to be had."

On our anniversary? I reminded him of the occasion. "Look," he said again, "it just isn't possible. But I do still have one hotel to hear from. They said they might have a suite, but it's a long way from downtown. Come on to my place and pick me up and I'll let you know then if I've heard from the Last Chance Hotel when I see you."

I approached the prospect with great apprehension. We had been on the road about 18 hours straight. And a suite in Chicago? On a PFC's pay?

When he came to get in the car he was beaming.

"The Windemere East has a suite they're holding for you. Let's go right now."

"Just for laughs, how much is it?"

"Normally, more than you can afford. But Chicago is a wonderful town for soldiers, and they have special rates for servicemen. They're going to close off the living room of the suite and give you the bedroom for $5 a night."

I was overjoyed. It wasn't the cheapest hotel I would rent in Chicago during my posting in Madison (that was $3.89 for the *night at the Palmer House), but it was certainly the best for the money and the occasion, a beautiful room in a beautiful hotel when we needed one bad.*

"Where shall we celebrate this anniversary?" I asked Mackey.

"I'd suggest the Tiger Room of the Sherman. Lots of servicemen go there, and it stays open pretty late. The food's fair if expensive, and the exotic drinks are famous all over town."

There was a reason the exotic drinks were so famous. They powered them up and challenged the soldiers to finish them. And the servicemen, of course, challenged the bartenders to fill them up again. After a late dinner an underclad girl with a camera took our pictures and gave them to us before we left. They confirmed what I already knew. The exotic drinks had won the battle, especially with Lt. Mackey. His eyes were wonderfully crossed and he looked like his head was about to hit the table. A solicitous MP approached him as we made our way to the men's room. He seemed to want to take care of the Lieutenant right there, finding him some comfortable drunk tank in the neighborhood where he could spend the night. Mackey has always been a little aggressive, and this was one of his finest hours. He not only gave the MP a large piece of his mind, he challenged him to a duel right in the hallway. I hastily pulled him off and got the MP to give him into my custody. We left the Tiger Room shortly thereafter. Mackey got in the back seat and promptly went to sleep. When we got to his housing, we dug him out, put him inside the door, which locked behind him, and fled. He was at least safe from the MPs.

Back at the Windemere East, there was no garage for the car so we locked it and left it on the street close to the hotel. Then we went in, claimed the key to our truncated suite, and fell into bed.

Next morning we got up reasonably early, had breakfast downstairs, took our overnight bags that were all we had brought into the hotel, and went to our car. The right rear window was shattered. Inside we could see my duffel bag and soldier clothing, but Marion's bags, with all the precious trousseau she had been so looking forward to wearing finally, were gone. She had only the light summer dress she had worn from Houston.

Rationing was in full force, of course. Gas, meat, sugar, flour, shoes, dresses, nylons if they could be found at all, everything had its little coupon in the time-restricted book they passed out with great care to the consumers. Marion's Dad had a special "C" rating on the gas rationing which gave him more than enough gas to manage his food warehousing operation in Houston. He made sure we would have enough gas. But otherwise it was just get by the best you could. Marion needed coupons for new shoes, for her dresses and all her underwear and stockings, for the suitcases themselves that were stolen. And of course, we also needed money to buy replacements for all the items she had lost.

I turned around and went back in to the Windemere and reported the burglary to the desk, who informed the local police. Then I called Dad in Shreveport to see if my property was insured under the circumstances. He informed me it was and promised to have the claim paid promptly. In the meantime I could borrow from him. Marion called her Dad and he assured her that he could find another shoe coupon to send her, but of course it wouldn't get to her for a few days. We went by the ration board and explained our predicament to them, calling on the hotel and the police report to prove our case. They were very understanding and immediately issued her an emergency shoe coupon. We bought a new pair of shoes for her and then decided we'd wait for Madison to get the rest.

We ultimately received $200 from the insurance money. Marion's sister Carol, then approaching 11 years old, thought that sounded wonderful. "Think of having $200 just to spend on clothes," she exclaimed. "What could be better!"

We proceeded on to Madison, broken window and all. As we went north, it became increasingly cooler, and the wind whistled through the shattered window. Inside Wisconsin we found a wonderful little café/bar with a crackling fire going. We stopped and warmed ourselves, had a refreshment, and went ahead. When we reached Madison it was 32°.

We checked into a downtown hotel for the night. The next morning we went to a nearby real estate office and asked about apartments to rent, preferably close to the university. June Simpson, the realtor on duty, told us the pickings were very slim, but she had one she could show us. Then she looked at Marion, shivering in her light summer dress. "Aren't you cold?" she asked. Marion nodded numbly. "Freezing," she said.

I explained the circumstances, that we were going to go shopping as soon as we could, but she said Marion had to put something else on. "I've got two coats here," she explained, "You can use one of them until you find a coat you like."

June and her husband Paul, who was in Madison in the Air Force, became our closest friends all during our nine months in ASTP. We never forgot her hospitality to a lost summer sparrow in the cold early fall in Wisconsin. She and Paul were from Marblehead, Massachusetts. She took us around that day and showed us Madison. In particular, she showed us 257 Langdon Street, a block from the University campus. It was a narrow, high wooden structure, four floors of it, looking like something out of *Anne of Green Gables.*

"Darbo [her realtor employer] has a couple of things here, if you'd like to look at them," she said. "They're on the top floor."

"Sounds good," I commented. "Let's take a look. Where is the elevator?"

She looked at me oddly. "There is no elevator. You only have to walk up three flights."

"Come on, Marion," I said. "Let's see how good condition we're in."

We huffed and puffed up the three flights and found ourselves in a wide, open hall. There were four doors leading off the hall. One obviously went to a bathroom right in front of us, one to a kitchen to the right looking out onto a girls' dormitory. The other two seemed to be entrances to bedrooms.

"Is there a door to this attic, or can anybody just come in?" Marion was obviously not too taken with it. I noticed a minute frown on June's forehead at the word "attic".

"How much is it?" I asked. I didn't figure we needed to keep it forever.

"It's $30 a month for each of the bedrooms. The kitchen and the bathroom are available to each tenant."

I strode around looking it over. I didn't like the idea of sharing it with another couple. "How much for the whole thing?"

"For the whole thing? Well, I don't know that I've ever heard Darbo quote a price for the whole thing as one unit, but I think he'd probably give it to you for $50 a month."

"Any lease?"

"No lease – month to month."

"We'll take it," I announced decisively. I heard a sharp intake of breath from Marion.

"Without a door to the fourth floor?" she murmured to herself. "With the girls' dormitory in full view outside the kitchen window? And there must be a reason for all these antique fire extinguishers sitting around. And..."

"You don't want to look at anything else?" June asked.

"Is there anything else this close to the University?" I hastened to seize the initiative in the conversation before Marion's unspoken questions became vocal.

"No."

"Then we'll take it. When can we move in?"

"Why...now, I guess. If you're ready."

"Lady," I said, "we're ready."

We made the front room, which was the larger of the two "bedrooms", into a living room. There were two fold-out couches for anticipated guests. The springs were very tight and if you hit them the wrong way they could come close to impaling you, but maybe they'd encourage the guests not to overstay. The other room was a comfortable bedroom looking out over a green yard with a large tree. The bathroom was a bathroom, nothing

21

more, with all the necessaries but none of the fineries. The kitchen was equipped for real cooking and had a fairly large breakfast table from which we could look out the window and wave to the girls in the dorm...and through which they could look back at us and whistle at me if I forgot and came into the kitchen in my underwear.

We were happy in 257 Langdon. I could run back to my "barracks" on campus when I had to, and it was close enough that I could come over for just a few minutes any time I thought I could get away with it. We became good friends with two other couples who lived at 257: Evelyn and Phil Durrell from Maine and Bob and Alice Barnecoat from Boston. And we continued to see June and Paul Simpson. All from New England and all doing time in the Services. Of course, the other couples didn't have the grand quarters we had, but then they didn't have to climb the three flights to the "attic", since they lived on the ground floor. Besides, their apartments had doors.

Truax Field was located on the other side of Madison, and a number of our friends and acquaintances were there from time to time. David McLure, Brown's brother, was there for a good while; even Marion's brother Tommy was there briefly. They both came and tried out the hard-spring couches and found it possible to sleep on them. Other guests came, too: Mother and Dad, Marion's Mom and Dad and Carol; Aunt Jane Ingersoll from Green Bay, Maybell Smith (Harris), and others. Their experiences with the couches was not quite as happy. But it was, nevertheless, something of a social center, 257 Langdon. My time there was not very much like being in the Army, but I didn't object.

Our unit, SU (for Special Unit) 3654, ASTP Company F, Barracks 11, University of Wisconsin, Madison, Wisconsin, was supposedly run like an Army outfit. But of course it wasn't. The Captain in charge, whose name is lost to history, was, believe it or not, a *horse cavalry* officer. He didn't bring his horse with him, but that's the only thing he didn't bring. He wore a stiff-brimmed round cavalry field hat with chin strap,

22

dressed in tight-fitting khakis with jodhpur-crafted pants, brightly shined boots – and he carried a swagger stick at all times, which he popped ominously against his jodhpurs to emphasize almost everything he said. On the rare occasions when we would march, he would give his orders as if he were leading a cavalry patrol: "Forward, Ho-o-o-o," and that sort of thing. He was about 5 feet 6 and rather portly, not particularly well suited for tight-fitting khakis. He sported an upper lip mustache which he had to watch constantly that it didn't develop into a Hitler mustache. He was a comical man, obviously frustrated and more unhappy at his command than we were to have him as our commander, fretting all the time that he was not out on the line – with his horse, I presume.

I was supposed to be in, as everyone was, every night except when we had passes. I was almost never in. The Captain was aware of this and let me know that he was playing the game but would catch me out one day. He chided me on breaking the rules, but all the time there was a smile playing around his eyes, as though he would probably do the same thing if his wife lived two blocks away. He would spring surprise inspections, coming to my room first of all. I had a great group of co-conspirators. My room-mate would tell him I was studying in someone else's room. The Captain would go galloping off to catch me, but the occupant would tell him I just left to go to another room. My room-mate would call me at 257 Langdon, and I would dash out the door, run the two blocks to the campus, and make a bee-line for my room. The Captain, meantime, would have been directed to room after room, always arriving to learn that I had just left, until finally the last referral, having been informed that all was well now, would direct him to my own room, where he would find me studying ferociously.

This happened quite a few times. He never caught me.

I checked in to the unit the day after we rented 257 Langdon. Our first order of business was to be briefed in a large lecture hall, and then we were given questionnaires. A lot of information about our backgrounds was requested, including

23

what languages we had studied. Finally, a question asked, "What language would you like to study at the University of Wisconsin?"

What an odd thing to ask. My whole experience with the Army was that they never asked you what you would like to do. And if by chance they did and you bit and told them, they would laugh their heads off and tell you that was the one thing they'd never let you do. Besides, I was high priority Portuguese, remember? I would turn the tables on them. Knowing they would never give it to me, I wrote: "German".

The next day they handed out the section assignments. I was assigned to the German section. Unbelievable! So were two new friends I had met, John ("Murph") Murphy from New Jersey and George Collier from Minneapolis. Another new acquaintance, Wolf Goeltzer, a native German-speaker, was assigned to Portuguese, presumably to take my place in that high-priority group.

The training was very rigorous. I think the educators at the University of Wisconsin wanted to develop a new system for teaching languages. It has since been widely taught as "immersion", but in those days it was new. We spent something like 40 hours a week at first in being beat over the head with German conversation. We weren't given any written materials, nor were we told the meaning of what we were saying. We were just instructed to say what we heard from the leaders, over and over again until we got the accent and the timing down in perfect imitation. *"Wo geht es hier zum Bahnhof?"* we would chant. *"Wie kommt mann nach Stuttgart?"* *"Wo ist die toilette, bitte?"* *"Nein, dass kommt später an die Reihe."* This latter became a source of great amusement when we were ultimately given the meanings of what we had been saying: "No, that comes later on the list." Everyone said it (in German) every chance he had. Marion heard us so much she learned it too, and when I would ask her if we were going to a movie that night or some such question, she would come back at me: *"Nein, dass kommt später an die Reihe."* She spoke it with a beautiful Texas accent.

24

We enjoyed life in Madison. It was much more like being at Rice (or maybe more like Sewanee, with the play-military in which we engaged). I was away all day speaking German, but Marion made good friends and they found things to do. A good part of her time was spent doing the grocery shopping. Living with ration books was not easy; one had to plan. She found that if she hadn't enough "points" left to afford steak, the firemen from around the block, who had gotten to know her as she walked to the grocery store, would always take care of her deficiency. They were given big meat rations (and sugar, too) so they would be strong and able to protect all of us from fire. In view of our fourth-floor apartment in the wooden building, I was very supportive of this concept. But they had more than they needed, and little Southerners supporting their soldier-husbands were beyond their capacity to resist. They were always perfect gentlemen in their conversational visits with Marion, and they added greatly to the enjoyment of our duty in Madison. Of course, they weren't always around, like the time Marion was out of points and the only meat available without points was rabbit. She brought a large one home, a very smelly thing, and we tried it – once. After that, she made sure there were some firemen in the store before she went.

I had a legitimate pass every week-end, from Saturday about 1:30 (depending on whether there was a football game or not) to Sunday night late. We drove the 150 miles into Chicago almost every week-end, using up Marion's Dad's gasoline coupons like mad. We stayed at $5 hotels in the lap of luxury, rode streetcars and buses free since I was in uniform, got free tickets at the USO (United Servicemen's Organization) to the best of Chicago's theaters and museums and ball games, and ate at Chicago's best restaurants for a pittance. Chicago was a great city for servicemen; it was almost less expensive than staying home – and more fun!

We came home on furlough in December and again in early June. I listened on the radio at Mother and Dad's house to the news of the Normandy invasion; we knew my older brother

Clyde was in the thick of it, landing at Omaha Beach with the 29th Division. All we could find out about the bloody invasion was that casualties were enormous, particularly on Omaha. Finally we received a cable that let us all breathe again. He had survived the beach but took a sniper's bullet in his leg on D+7. Ultimately he was sent home to a hospital in Jackson, Mississippi. For his actions on the beach, he was awarded the Distinguished Service Cross. He was a true hero.

Coming home on furlough was always an experience. One was never sure he wouldn't be "bumped" by someone with a greater priority than a lowly private going home for a week on furlough. We would drive to Midway Airport (*O'Hare hadn't been built yet*), park the car and board the Chicago & Southern DC-3 southward bound, clutching our tickets tightly. We always survived the first stop, at St. Louis, but Memphis was another thing. We were bumped one time there. We had to dash to the railroad station and take the train to Texarkana, where we were met by one of the family. On the way back it would be the same lottery. There was a good aspect to it, though: I could always send a telegram that I had been bumped and would be late checking back in, and it was always accepted at face value.

It was cold in Madison over the winter, of course. But it wasn't nearly as cold as it usually was, all the natives told us, and I think that must have been true. We had very little snow, although the temperature usually made it down to the 0° level at night. The beautiful lakes sprinkled like a necklace around the city all froze over, and there was much skating on them. One Saturday I borrowed some skates of Tommy's (Marion's brother) sent from Houston for the occasion and took off with Marion (in her very own skates!) to glide effortlessly, we anticipated, across the lake. It was quite windy, and as expected we sailed along on the wings of the wind to the farther shore with little effort. When we started back, however, it was virtually impossible for us to make any headway, and we floundered around wasting our energy fruitlessly. I began to get really concerned, cold as it was, when we saw in the distance two expert skaters winging their way toward us in urgent search. It was Murph and George Collier, both northerners and both skaters – and they were a welcome sight. Murph took one of Marion's hands and George the other and they started off for home. I struggled along behind in the lee of their three bodies and we finally made it back, thoroughly exhausted. Good friends come in handy.

As the time went by, our German group began to really understand what it was all about. We spoke German to each other much of the time; we heard lectures on German culture – history, economics, Nazism, music, theater, soldiers' songs (*Ich hatt' einen Kamerad*), folk songs (*Du, du liegst mir im Herzen, du, du liegst mir im Sinn*), Nazi songs like the *Horst Wessel,* which almost converted me it was so emotionally commanding. We studied German military structure and history, came to know the *Afrika Korps,* Rommel ("the Desert Fox"), and von Rundstedt better than our own Army. After the first three months, most of our culture lectures were in German by native German speakers, and our ears became comfortably accustomed to the cadence and the accent. It was a wonderful program, well designed and well executed.

After each three-month trimester, we saw some of our group shipped out, we never knew where. But we suspected that, aside from the ones who were eliminated from the program, most of the German-speakers were headed for intelligence work of some variety. Military Intelligence Service (MIS) was headquartered and the personnel trained at Camp Ritchie, Maryland (where my brother Clyde had also trained). We began to concentrate on that possibility.

About the middle of March Marion returned from a visit to the obstetrician at Camp Truax and announced that our suspicions were confirmed: she was pregnant. We were both elated and apprehensive. When was the baby due? The latter part of November. Would I be around when it arrived? Who could know? Probably not.

27

Our elation soon overcame our apprehension. If I wasn't here, the baby would be, and Marion would have her time well used as she waited for me. She could live with her folks in Houston or mine in Shreveport, or some of both. With the increase in her monthly allotment because of the baby, she and the baby would grow rich while our families outfitted them, fed them, doctored them, and did everything else necessary. It wasn't perfect; I didn't want to be gone, but the positives outweighed the negatives enough to celebrate the news. The doctors' bills and the hospital charges would be taken care of by the government, which was quite generous on that score. Of course they weren't that generous to the doctors: the maximum fee for maternities was $35. Back in Houston, the old-line obstetrician told Marion he would rather treat her as a charity patient than go through all the red tape to get his $35 from the government. Marion accepted. But she paid his $100 bill when he forgot the deal.

We got our orders before we were given our final furlough in early June. I was being sent with the major contingency to Camp Ritchie, as expected. George Collier and Murph were in the same group; our El Paso friend, Francisco Licón, would be going elsewhere. His Mexican accent was a little much for the Germans. My friend Bessinger was already at Ritchie; his group had started before ours and he was half-way through the program.

Marion stayed in Houston until I could get to Ritchie. I would try to find a place for her to stay and then she would join us. Mother knew a good bit about the area, because she had been there with Clyde and his wife, Margie. She would help find something.

I returned to Madison and in due time boarded a composite troop train with all of my fellow Germans. It was going to a number of locations, the last of which was Ritchie. It was an un-airconditioned (and therefore open-windowed) coach train. We would be on it most of three days. The soot flew through the window almost constantly from the coal-burning engine, and by the time we arrived we were dirty, unwashed, exhausted from trying to sleep in coach seats not made for sleeping, and irritable. We looked around at our new home through tired and jaundiced eyes. Even with that, it was a splendid sight.

U S Army, Military Intelligence Hq
Camp Ritchie, Maryland
17 June 1944

The Blue Ridge Mountains are beautiful. The hills are green and rolling, not stony and craggy, and they are almost universally cultivated, mostly with apple and peach orchards. The Pennsylvania state line runs just to the north of the entrance to the camp, and a few miles down that road is the Victorian summer resort of Blue Ridge Summit, which used to be a very popular place for Washingtonians and Philadelphians to escape the summer heat. Now, with gasoline rationing, it's almost empty except for the families of the military in the area.

A little beyond Blue Ridge Summit is the town of Gettysburg, where the catastrophic civil war battle was fought and the Southern cause lost forever. To the west and down the mountain heights is the town of Hagerstown, Maryland, the administrative capital for the locality. The view from the heights toward Hagerstown is spectacular. Once down the mountain, the terrain becomes rolling and inviting. In the distance the rolling hills level out into a plain which seems to stretch to the Pacific Ocean. At sunset the sun performs its eternal task of creating a masterpiece of color and reflection. A number of summer cottages are built on the high point facing westward. The hour of sunset calls for an evening of calm relaxation with wine glass in hand. It is a place and time for quiet contemplation and the enjoyment of easy life. In normal times. But these are not normal times, and the beauty of the mountain, the rolling hills, the plain and the brilliant sunsets is dirtied by the purpose to which we must put them now. The ugliness of war makes the beauty almost obscene.

We will be here something over eight weeks. That's the length of the course; how much beyond that will depend on when and how we will be going overseas. This is the last U. S. point for the lads in this camp, including us – unless we get booted out after four weeks because we're not making the grade

30

for any reason. Then it would be back to some AA replacement battalion somewhere, I guess. I don't intend to let that happen.

There are several kinds of disciplines being taught at Ritchie. Photo Interpretation (PI) is one – inspecting in depth aerial photographs to determine the position and size and orientation of items on the ground – command posts, gun emplacements, tanks, troop dispositions, even the identification of the troops and their units. The binocular pictures from which they work are similar to the old binocular scenes we used to look at through the device we held up to our eyes. Remember how they gave us a sense of three-dimensions? The PI people do the same sort of thing, looking through a little stand with lenses and training their eyes to look straight ahead individually instead of focusing together. It's amazing what a trained observer can tell from the exercise. Bessinger is in photo interpretation.

Then there is the Order of Battle discipline. This involves memorizing German unit statistics and their commanders, histories, strengths, and weaknesses. The Order of Battle changes constantly, and the practitioner must keep track of changes in the order from time to time. Collier, from Madison, and a new friend, Gene Golan of Chicago, are in that discipline. Gene's new wife, Maxine, will also be living in Blue Ridge Summit while we are at Ritchie, and I imagine Marion and she will get together.

There are other disciplines, but the major one is that in which I find myself: the Interrogation of Prisoners of War. Murph is in that discipline also, and we shall see a great deal of one another over the next eight weeks, at least. The purpose of interrogation at "field" level is to extract from prisoners taken by our forces information about the Order of Battle, the men in command of units in front of the unit served by the IPW team, the history of those units, who belongs to them, where they came from and when, where they trained, what kind of arms and armor they have. Of most interest to the commanders down the line (regiments, battalions, companies, etc.), are the positions of crucial armaments, headquarters, machine gun emplacements,

31

locations of the justly famous 88-mm Pak-Flak artillery piece, and so forth.

The prisoners are not expected to cooperate with us just because we ask them too. The rules of war provide that they must divulge only name, rank and serial number. Nothing else. Our interrogations are supposed to break that wall of silence. The techniques used to "break" prisoners do not include resort to the physical. Only psychological. Only verbal persuasion. It's OK to threaten, within limits, or to lead them to cooperation by means of scenarios which seldom are truthful. It is similar to a cross-examination of a witness with no opposing attorney to cry "Objection!" and with no holds barred short of physical assault. All for a good cause, but now perhaps you understand why I see the beautiful hills dirtied by the teachings of war here.

The camp is filled not only with those of us in training, but with a motley-looking bunch of characters dressed in shabby German uniforms and speaking almost entirely German. They are our "practice prisoners" whom we will have the task of interrogating and "breaking" in field simulation conditions. They are said to be Americans posing as German prisoners; I personally believe they are in fact German prisoners recruited for this job. That would be contrary to the rules of war also, and it wouldn't do for their sakes to have it believed abroad. I think they are covering as Americans for that reason. At any rate, when we are not interrogating them they are pleasant enough and it's hard to tell whether they are American or German because they always speak German anyway.

We will have quite a lot of field exercises. Part of it will be simulated interrogations and actions based on the results of those interrogations: "war games" in miniature. One field problem lasts for 8 days and is called, reasonably enough, the "8-day problem". We will be in full field conditions for that time, chow, sleep, baths, marches and everything. The 8-day problem is regarded as the climax of our training and as a final chance to be weeded out of the system.

This is the Army, not school as in Madison. We are strictly controlled, a general obligation of secrecy overhangs the camp, and we are carefully checked in and out when we are on pass. I don't think I'll use my Shumate passes here. An AWOL would throw everything into reverse.

The Commanding General is named "Bann". He has devised a system for the granting of free time which has certain advantages and certain disadvantages. Instead of being off every Sunday or every Saturday and Sunday, we work for seven days running and then are off every 8th day. The free day is called a "Bann-day" in honor of its inventor. He gets more effectivity out of the program, but we get freedom for a day during the week, which opens up a lot of opportunities that might not be as easy to do on Sundays. It's better for the community because it spreads throughout the week the crowds of soldiers who would be clogging the system on Sundays otherwise. Whatever the advantages or disadvantages (the principal argument being, of course, that we get fewer days off in total), Banndays are a fact of life and will not change while we are here. We must learn to live with them.

Marion arrived about ten days after I got here. She and Granny drove up from Houston and Shreveport together. I had found a room for her in a pleasant and clean house in Blue Ridge Summit, which is fine except that there is nothing for her to do there. Also, one of the previous co-owners of the house hanged herself some time ago in the basement, which casts something of a pall over the ambiance. An answer to the quarters question, but probably not a permanent one.

As an appendage to the Ritchie Officers' Club, there is a nice man-made lake in which swimming is encouraged. There is a problem, though: Enlisted Men and their families are not permitted. This hurts Marion's feelings as well as depriving her of the opportunity to lie in the pale sun of the mountains and swim in the cold waters of the lake. This would be very welcome, since there is of course no air conditioning in the house in Blue Ridge Summit. For the first time in my life, I suppose, I have a faint understanding of the problems of living as a second class citizen. The sandy shores of the lake are sparsely populated most days. There is plenty of room for the wives of the Enlisted Men. But the sign says "Officers Only." And they mean it.

Time passes quickly at Ritchie. Activity is intense. There is a reality about the exercise that portends a serious future different from the easy game-playing of my Army career thus far. For the first time I have a clear concept of how I might make a real difference in this great battle against cruelty, oppression and injustice. I am glad that my serial number begins with a digit that indicates I enlisted rather than was drafted. I am proud to be a part of the war that needs to be fought.

Marion has met Maxine Golan and, despite their geographic and cultural background differences, they get along fine. They decide to share accommodations, and begin to hunt for a suitable place. They find a summer home perched on the mountainside looking toward Hagerstown and strike a deal with the realtor for it. Soon they move in and Mother comes to join them. She helps, too — the hot water heater is wood burning, and we bow to her expertise on how to build a successful wood fire. Gene Golan's only problem has been that there is never any hot water when he gets a pass to spend a night at home. Mother solves that and he thinks she is wonderful.

We march past the house on a field trip, early one morning. The morning mists are still swirling around the mountain and the house is sleepily quiet. Our feet crunch the gravel of the road, but otherwise the column keeps silent. I try whistling a tune Marion will know, in hopes that she may come to the window, but she sleeps on and my march carries me quickly past. Never mind – it's still good to know she's just down the road even if I don't get to see her. The baby, now five months in gestation, grows without any real prenatal help from the medical profession. Its time will come, as indeed so will mine.

Finally, the eight weeks are over. We are divided into teams. For Interrogation of Prisoners of War Team 138, our table of organization calls for a Captain, a Lieutenant, a Master Sergeant, two Staff Sergeants (Tec 3s) and one Tec 5, a rank equivalent to Corporal. But we only get two Lieutenants, a Staff Sergeant, two Tec 3s and the Tec 5. I am to be the Staff Sergeant. The senior Lieutenant and I will have to earn the rest of our allotted rank.

The "Captain" in our team is George D. Buxbaum. He's somewhere in his 30s, a member of a prominent Jewish family in Czechoslovakia which owns textile factories in the Silesian textile centers of the far northeast of the country. He has had no news of his family for years. He attended the University of Berlin and later lived in Belgium. He speaks Czech, Polish, German, Russian, French and English with fluency. He came to America in his twenties, I believe, and has been working with an uncle and other family members in the importation of fine linens and other textiles. He is quite urbane and handsome and likes the finer things of life. He doesn't have much to do with the Enlisted Men, me included.

The Lieutenant in the team is of English descent and has family in England. His name is Holmes, like the famous detective. He seems to be all right, but I don't know much more about him than that.

The others on the team include Phil Levine of Boston, and Herb Schick of St. Louis as our "Tec 3s" and a Tec 5 named Raubitschek, whom I know only slightly. Phil and Herb are both high-profile Jewish. Phil was born and grew up in America, but his family is definitely German Jewish and Phil apparently was raised a strict Jew. His family speaks Yiddish and German (which are of course quite similar) and his command of German is very good. His family sends him Kosher salamis and other food to encourage him to observe the dietary laws. He finds that very difficult to do on Army routine.

Schick lived most of his life in Austria but was born in New York City, a happy accident of fate. He is also Jewish, but not nearly so orthodox as Phil. His family was well aware of the danger of being Jewish in Austria at the time, and through the

35

American consulate in Vienna they successfully claimed Herb's American heritage. This resulted in an exit permit in about 1938, the year of the *Anschlüss* of Austria and Germany, and he came to live with relatives in St. Louis. The rest of the family was not allowed to exit. He had one brother younger than he is, whose whereabouts or fate he doesn't know. He hasn't heard from any of his family in five or six years. Herb speaks German as a native, of course; his English is not perfect.

I stick out like a sore thumb in the team, a White Anglo Saxon Protestant (a WASP) by every criterion. But almost from the start I begin to understand my role. The others are there to interrogate in their native or almost native language. I am there to write up the results of their work in language that our commanders can understand. I am the English-writer of the group. My typing skill, such as it is, is a big part of my qualification.

Murph is also assigned to an IPW team, I believe largely for the same reason that I have been named to my position. His team will travel with us. Collier and Golan are assigned in Order of Battle and our paths will diverge. Bessinger was assigned to Photo Interpretation and I will not see much of him either.

We are ordered to Camp Kilmer, New Jersey for shipment overseas. We will pick up our extensive equipment and supplies there and at our destination. We are not told any specific date when we will sail, and of course we are not supposed to talk about it anyway. Marion and Mother move into New York to stay with our cousins, the Frank Andrews (Manager of the New Yorker Hotel in Manhattan) until we leave. They hope I will be given passes to come in until we sail. I share their hope.

Our days of preparation are approaching their end. Now we will go to war.

The Stuff of War

Excerpts from the Bad Meinberg Letters

Jim Hargrove

15 May 1945
Bad Meinberg, Land Lippe
G E R M A N Y

I have been challenging myself for some time, as soon as censorship regulations eased, to write recapitulating the story of our wanderings over the Atlantic, England, and the Continent in pursuit of the war. I begin that task now. How long it will take, I do not know.

After my last visit in New York with you early Monday morning, 25 September 1944, I went down to the bus station off Times Square, waited in line for my ticket to Camp Kilmer, got it, and fought my way onto a bus, which, of course, was crowded to the roof. I managed to find a place and settled down for an hour's sleep. Back at the camp, I very sleepily found my way to the barracks and slept for another two hours. The rest of the day was very uneventful, except the men who got passes that day got them three hours ahead of the scheduled time, giving them actually 15 hours off instead of the 12 which they were supposed to get. Consequently, I felt very good about my chances for a long pass the next day.

Of course the next day, about 9 a.m., we were alerted. That was the end of the pass.

That final alert gave me a very sinking feeling, which I remember only once before having experienced in the Army, and that was when I was let off at Camp Beauregard that Sunday afternoon in February 1943 to report for active duty. That time I didn't know how long it would be before I saw you again, nor where I would be going, and I felt pretty empty. This time, though, I knew that it would be a very long time before I saw you again, and the fact that I knew in a general sort of way where I was going didn't help the situation a bit. The feeling was quite a bit sinkier than the Beauregard feeling. Not that I hadn't been expecting it...I knew of course, as everybody else did, that the every-other-day passes wouldn't last forever and that sooner or later we would be shoving off, but that also didn't

39

alleviate matters. I wanted, naturally, to get word to you that I wouldn't be in Tuesday night, but it was absolutely impossible, so I didn't even try.

The rest of Tuesday, and all of Wednesday and most of Thursday, we were busy with final packing and readying everything for departure. We were well loaded down when we boarded the train Thursday night with full packs, overcoats, duffel bags, musette bags, gas masks, our "grease gun" automatic pistols, and all the other miscellaneous paraphernalia that we had to carry along. Just when I thought I had everything conceivable, they gave me a portable typewriter to carry also. The train was, as can be imagined, very crowded, and it wasn't too comfortable a trip to Hoboken, where we detrained and piled onto a ferry to cross the Hudson River. Comfort, however, wasn't expected by anyone, and although there was much griping and the like, no one really cared whether he was very comfortable for the time or not. When we got on the ferry, we didn't know if we were going to Manhattan or Brooklyn, and wagers were flying everywhere. On the basis of some "inside dope", I risked a dollar that it was Brooklyn. I lost the dollar. We were headed for a pier on about 45th Street, Manhattan.

At the pier we disembarked from the ferry and lined up under a shed to all the attendant ceremony and confusion usually associated with such affairs. The band was playing something (not a march or military music, I was surprised to hear, but swing), and there were Red Cross women there with coffee, doughnuts, and apparently millions of chocolate bars which they forced on us at regular thirty second intervals. While waiting to embark, I got my first look at the ship – a 10,000 ton Scotch freighter remodeled to serve as a troop transport, and looking very small to take the multitude of soldiers who were waiting to board. This impression, I suppose, was furthered by the rumors which had been circulating before about the Queen Elizabeth, the Queen Mary, the Acquitania, and other large ships in harbor at the time just waiting to carry us personally across.

40

The name appearing on the bow of our ship informed us that home for the next week or so was to be the S. S. Cilicia.

Ultimately we all got aboard, staggering slightly up the gangplank under the load of all the items I mentioned previously, and clutching in two free fingers or sometimes in our mouths the little red tickets which informed us we were quartered in Troop Compartment D-3, a designation which meant, I found out quickly, we were in a compartment amidships on the third deck below the main deck. Not the choicest spot, but certainly not the worst, as I discovered the first time I looked in at the boys in D-5, stuck way down in the stern hold right behind the diesel engines. Our compartment was, if a little crowded, well ventilated and clean enough. The bunks were stacked three deep, and I, through no choice of my own, got the lower in one tier. Since I couldn't turn sidewise in my bunk, however, it didn't really make any difference – at least Murphy, who was right above me, wasn't heavy enough to stretch the bunk disproportionately, so I still had two or three inches of clearance above my nose.

After we got settled and more or less straightened out, Murph and I went up on deck to have a look at the skyline and bid New York goodbye. It was just about midnight, Thursday, 28 September 1944, and I remember I could just make out the outline of the New Yorker Hotel off to the right. I wondered then if you were still there, and wished I had a carrier pigeon or something to send you a note, but it was all in vain – all I could do was look.

Soon we introduced ourselves to the ship's washing and sanitary facilities (which were, to say the least, quaint, but which, in view of what I have since seen, I have come to regard as comparatively luxurious). Then we retired for the night.

The next morning when we awoke we discovered that we were already standing off the New Jersey coast, so that we could just see the hills of the coastline in the distance. Breakfast was somewhat of a nightmare of waiting in line only to be disappointed at what you had been waiting for, and it took the

41

major part of the morning just to get it. During the day, the convoy slowly, almost imperceptibly, formed and got under way. By night we were fully at sea, accompanied by quite a few other small troopships, a covey of destroyers (who were most of the time way out on the horizon), and several small aircraft carriers.

The Cilicia was manned entirely with Scottish personnel. It had seen plenty of action before it was converted to a troopship. The voice of the ship's officer which used to come over the loud speaker system was very Scottish, and the way he used to drag out his "Attention, all perrr-sonnel" and "Emerrr-gency stations" at boat drills we thought very reminiscent of the highlands, or the lowlands, or some part of Scotland, which none of us had ever seen. We were to learn later, though, that the man spoke the very King's English in comparison to the real Scot tongue.

Boat drills were the highlight on most days, except when they interrupted a bridge game or caught me in the middle of a book. They were the only times we got any exercise, and it was exercise, to scramble up the ladders and gangways, cursing the man ahead of you for going so slow and cursing the man behind you for telling you to hurry up. The fastest time for Emergency Stations was, I think, three minutes, which wasn't too good and wasn't too bad, considering all the people on the ship and the lack of space into which to put them.

We were preparing ourselves against a submarine attack, which was a real possibility. The destroyers on the perimeter of the convoy and all the other ships between the perimeter and the troopships were our defense against attack. Several times during the trip we could see ships with plumes of smoke, obviously on the losing end of a battle with submarines. We never had anything close to us. A good thing. Someone asked what we should do if we were hit. The response was to get in the lifeboats and prepare to be launched. But what if the lifeboats are full, another asked. "Then jump in the bloody ocean and swim as fast away from the ship as you can. A boat may be able to pick you up…and don't forget to wear your lifejacket."

"How long can we last in the water before we freeze?" a third asked.

"You'll have about 35 seconds in the North Atlantic at this time of year," came the final reply. No one asked any more questions.

The voyage seemed to me to be endless. It was completely uneventful, and the boredom was broken for me for only one day, when I was sick. During that time I would infinitely have preferred to be bored rather than sick. I never was really sick to the extent that some people get seasick, but I felt uneasy enough to wish it would go away.

The plays – to treat the subject kindly – which I along with some other volunteers put on for various compartments in the ship, were certainly not good. The only thing entertaining about them was the free cigarettes which we gave away to keep the people watching. I thought I would enjoy doing the plays – I had been in almost every Rice Dramatic Society offering – but they were just too dreadful. One performance I did enjoy, one for the officers, where I experienced great satisfaction in watching a Major make a fool of himself trying to light a cigarette with boxing gloves on. Even more I relished breaking up a poker game which several Majors had casually continued playing during the performance. I had the band play the "Star Spangled Banner" and they all had to stand up...

After about a week at sea we all started looking around for land to come into sight. As a result, the three or four days more than a week before we docked were longer than the rest of the trip put together. Finally, though, we did sight a piece of land – an island – and made a sharp turn northwards, from which we deduced that we must be swinging around the southern coast of Ireland. At that move we decided the rumor that we were to land in France was unfounded. As we steamed north (or rather dieseled north) into the Irish Sea, we began to lose parts of the convoy. When we ultimately turned into the Firth of Clyde and dropped anchor in the harbor there, we had only a few ships left. That was early morning of 10 October 1944. We were standing off Greenoch, Scotland. Glasgow was a short distance up the River Clyde.

Later that morning a detail was selected, which I got onto without knowing exactly what it was for, and through no fault of my own. I heard from many sources, though, that it was a very desirable detail, being an unloading group to proceed to Glasgow to take care of our unit's organizational equipment unloading. It was said that the detail might be in Glasgow for a week or ten days, and that passes were issued into town every night. When this news got around, everyone tried to get on the detail, and ultimately no one with a rank lower than Staff Sergeant was selected. I was still on it – I liked the idea of visiting Glasgow myself.

Some ten men from our outfit boarded a barge to go up the river, in more ways than one, that afternoon. We got our first taste of weather in the United Kingdom. It was cold and raining and not at all pleasant. When we reached Glasgow, we were taken to the Transit Camp (an old gymnasium where they were putting up untold numbers of men under one large roof) and received an "indoctrination" talk. It was an unhappy lecture.

"Passes," we were told by a Lieutenant we all took an instant dislike to, "are non-existent since day before yesterday. Twenty-five men were court-martialed yesterday for violation of this order, and any further violations will be dealt with similarly. You may not leave the confines of this building except to be transported to the docks for your work there, at the conclusion of which you will be returned here."

The situation was ruefully discussed at length and in none too polite words. We all agreed that we had made a mistake of large dimension to get on a detail which threatened us with another week or ten days' confinement after having been that long on the boat. All the while, in our minds' eyes we could see the boys who had gone on, hear them laughing at us, imagine them enjoying passes to London, Liverpool and every other city in the British Isles. It was not a comforting picture.

We soon found out, too, that when the gentleman said "work", that is what he meant. Although we had ostensibly come to unload only our own organizational equipment, we discovered that actually we were mixed in with other groups and the whole bunch was treated as one, working on all the cargo that happened to come in while we were there. We acted as longshoremen, taking the cargo out of the barges (using the dock cranes for this job, thank goodness), sorting it into piles for the units for whom it was intended, and then loading the assorted freight onto the little toy boxcars they use in England. As the members of our detail were all staffs or higher, we naturally got the foreman jobs, but some of those necessitated working with the men, too, and that was no gold-brick proposition.

For three days we worked in this fashion, utilizing our lunch hour to get our only glimpses of Glasgow and our only tastes of the Scottish dew. We found the Scots very friendly to us, and more than once the age-old concept of the stinginess of the Scots was repudiated by the offer of a free beer. I cannot say that I found Glasgow charming or pretty, but I must admit in all fairness that I saw only the waterfront, and I doubt whether the waterfront of any harbor city in the world is pretty.

We left Glasgow after only three or four days, in which I consider we were very lucky. Why we left so soon I don't really know, unless it was the fact that our organizational equipment amounted to nothing more than five or six pyramidal tents plus pegs, and the fact that so many high-ranking non-coms embarrassed the officers, who didn't seem to be accustomed to such rank. The Master Sergeant in charge of our detail, who was made acting First Sergeant of the Transit Camp during our stay, told the officers a few times what he thought of some of their regulations, and I think it intimidated them.

Anyway, we left Glasgow on 15 October 1944, if I'm not mistaken, traveling by ourselves by rail to our next destination, which was to be Lichfield Station, near Birmingham. The rail journey was most uninteresting, being at night where we couldn't see anything of the countryside. The next morning we arrived in Lichfield, having changed trains twice en route. When we pulled into the 10th Replacement Depot outside of Lichfield, the first persons we saw were two teams which had been separated from the group back in Camp Ritchie because their assigned units needed them immediately. It was assumed that they would fly to Europe . They had not – as a matter of fact they had stayed in the States longer than we had, had come over on a more comfortable ship, and had made a quicker crossing than we had. We had a joyful reunion with them all, among whom incidentally was Wolf Goeltzer. He was to encounter the only real piece of bad luck of any of the gang from Ritchie about whom I have heard, and now he is no longer with us in the land of the living. He was the one with whom I had been the longest, as he was with me at A & M, then all through ASTP at Wisconsin, and later at Ritchie. His team was assigned to the 106th Infantry Division, ordered to Europe to replace a veteran division. Goeltzer and his team had to wait on the Division; it didn't reach Europe on schedule.

We stayed at the 10th Replacement Depot for lunch and then late in the afternoon – as a matter of fact, right as it was getting dark – we were put into trucks and sent to Pheasy Farms, an annex of the 10th Depot some miles away, but connected to Birmingham with frequent bus service. There, at Pheasy, we found the rest of our IPW group. It was pitch dark when we pulled into the place, and we had the dickens of a time lugging all of our equipment around until we finally found the house we were supposed to stay in. Pheasy had been a housing project for workers in Birmingham, but it was never quite finished because of the war. As quarters, it was not bad, and its proximity to Birmingham made it basically a nice place to be.

Basically was all, though. We soon found out that the boys at the Depot (that is, the cadre there) didn't care for us very much. Perhaps that is easily understood when one realizes that most of them were veterans, with Purple Hearts and such, and they resented seeing a bunch coming fresh from the States with as much rank as we had. But it wasn't so bad after the first few days. Most of us got passes to Birmingham quite often, and when we didn't, it was easy enough to dodge the MPs at the first bus stop and catch it at the second. Once in Birmingham no one ever asked for passes, and we were allowed to be anywhere on post during the night, so for a bunch such as we were, "specialists" from Ritchie, it was a simple and almost natural matter to avoid detection when traveling without a pass.

Some 24-hour passes were given out – true, not as many as to the regular inmates of the Depot, who received a couple a week if they stayed at the place long enough – but still enough. When we first got there, we were told that anyone who had relatives in England could apply for a pass, with those having mothers, fathers, brothers, sisters, etc., getting preference. Under such circumstances, of course, the number of cousins and uncles which people suddenly realized they had in England rose amazingly. I myself reasoned that Jess Bessinger was almost like a cousin, and he was supposed to be in London, according to what I had last heard from him. So I filed application under that reasoning. The boys who really had relatives would get the passes first, anyhow, and I was quite sure that Bessinger was just as much my cousin as 99% of the cousins that were springing up through the outfit.

In due time, which is to say in four or five days, I got my pass to London, along with Dick Kroner, who had borrowed an address in London from someone to think up a cousin. We didn't have much time there – the train was late, of course, and when I got to town it was already beginning to get dark. I lost Kroner on the subway from the train station to Piccadilly Circus, where we were going to register with the Red Cross for a place to stay. Kroner met an old friend of his on the subway (he had known her for at least two or three minutes) and she offered to show him some of the sights in London town. I remembered the old adage that three is sometimes considered an excessive number of persons under such circumstances, and journeyed on alone. I registered with the Red Cross, managed to see a show (which was very mediocre), ate a mediocre dinner, and slept in a very comfortable bed with clean sheets, etc. Next morning I got up early, managed to see Westminster Abbey and the Parliament buildings (although I couldn't go in the latter because there was no official tour at that time) and went back to the station, where I met Kroner again and we returned to Pheasy. On the return trip the train was once more late, and we overstayed our passes a little, but nothing happened.

My other 24-hour pass was to Stratford-on-Avon, which was very much more satisfactory than the London trip. For one thing, it was much closer and we had more time to spend, so I got to see a lot more of the sights, including Shakespeare's tomb, Anne Hathaway's cottage, and Shakespeare's birthplace (although it was closed by the time we got there and we could only give it a cursory inspection). We bicycled to Warwick where we looked over the grounds of the Warwick Castle and visited all the old villages along the way. The Red Cross club in Stratford was very nice, and we managed to get a pretty nice dinner at one of the restaurants there. We also had an interesting conversation with a communistically inclined WAAF on the way back. A very educational trip.

On my short passes to Birmingham (with Murphy most of the time) I saw several Shakespearean plays and a couple of others, witnessed a game of soccer, which I found interesting but no match for our football, formed a casual acquaintance with several pubs in the town, became accustomed but not reconciled to warm beer, and, within limits, enjoyed myself.

That was the good side of the stay at Pheasy. The other, and therefore bad, side was the continual pettiness and attitude of the cadre which we had to put up with. We were alerted several times before we finally left the place, and every time we were alerted we had one or more "show-down inspections". Now a showdown inspection, in case you are not familiar with the term, involves displaying each and every little thing which you own to an inspector, who on occasions such as these, where the inspection was allegedly prior to shipment to the continent, checked off what you had against a list of allowables. The list against which we were checked was for infantry replacements, which was what the Depot handled almost exclusively. It stands to reason that an infantryman, and especially a replacement, cannot take as much as a member of an intelligence team which has two jeeps and a trailer for six men. This aspect of the question, however, did not enter the picture, except when it was brought to the attention of the inspecting officers by one of our group. Then the inspecting officer became very angry and threatened to court-martial the next man who mentioned it. In the show-down we were stripped mercilessly of a large majority of the clothing and personal equipment which we had brought from the States. The majority of the bunch, of course, being Ritchie "specialists", was well trained in the art of deception and camouflage, and when we ultimately left the place I daresay almost everyone had more than he arrived with.

Some of us did get things taken away. A major bone of contention in this respect was the question of civilian shoes, which almost everybody had. I personally lost mine, partly because I was careless enough not to hide them, and partly because I figured I wouldn't need them anymore. I wish I had them now, though. It was always a question of what became of the confiscated shoes, and I must admit that the consensus among us was that someone in the cadre was making a nice sum retailing the shoes to the English, who were in desperate need of them. In the matter of the show-downs, our officers took no part, which we thought was rather inexcusable, because they should have protected us, but then they weren't subject to the inspection, so they didn't need to bother about it.

Our treatment as a very undesirable element continued for quite a while, finally being abandoned when the head of the Field Interrogation Division of MIS visited the Depot and interviewed each one of us personally for some special assignment. The gentleman in question being a full colonel made the cadre wonder for a while whether we *were* actually just infantry or not, and when we ultimately got in our quota of jeeps, trailers, and tons of equipment, they must have decided that we were telling the truth about our transportation facilities, because we didn't have any more show-down inspections by them. Most of our affairs were handled from that time by our own officers.

Picking up our jeeps and trailers offered a break in routine for a few days. The trailers were down at a base ordnance plant, G-25, in the neighborhood of Gloucester, and we had to go down there and assemble them. The officer in charge was a darned nice fellow, and I was the NCO in charge, which made things easier. After we got back from G-25 with the trailers, we found that the first half of our jeeps had already been driven up from Bristol, where they had been off-loaded. A couple of days later a large detail set out for Cardiff to pick up and drive back the other half. I was on that detail, too, and again enjoyed it. We got the night off in Cardiff and I soaked up a little Welsh atmosphere. There I saw the first effects of bombing a city, as the whole center of the town had been leveled. The rubble had been cleared away, though, and it didn't look anything like the towns I later saw in France and especially in Germany. The next day we drove back in a convoy of 70 jeeps with no untoward incidents (which for that crowd, many of whom had learned to drive at Ritchie, was quite a feat).

The next few days were spent in feverish preparation, issuing equipment, packing it in the jeeps, and getting ready to leave. Early in the morning of 20 November 1944, we pulled out of Pheasy, bag and baggage. Not having heard yet of the baby, I knew it would be some time before the information would catch up to me, with all the moving around I envisioned in the next weeks. I was right; it was three weeks later that I heard the baby had been born four days after I left Pheasy.

19 May 1945
Bad Meinberg, Land Lippe
G E R M A N Y

When we pulled out of Pheasy Farms early that Monday morning, 20 November, it was cold as the dickens and, as usual, raining in the fine drizzle that was the most annoying feature of the English weather. A good solid rain I didn't mind so much, but the frequent steady drizzles were nerve-wracking.

We proceeded south through the English countryside in a long convoy of jeeps and trailers and arrived at our destination without accident or incident. Our new temporary home was Camp C 13, a marshaling area near the port of Southampton. It was a dreary, uninviting looking place consisting entirely of Nissen huts, than which there is no more disheartening sight. We lined the jeeps up and parked them, and then had to post a guard on them. The first night there I slept in the jeep when I wasn't pulling guard, and nearly froze to death. The next day I was through with guard and I secured a cot in one of the huts and slept for a few hours, once more warm. If we had known, incidentally, how valuable and handy those cots were, I think we would have left the place richer by several of them, even as we left Pheasy Estates richer by some number of English blankets which we had been given (without signing for them!) at that place. The story of the blankets, incidentally, was funny, and I understand there was quite a stink raised when it was discovered how drastically the blanket population had fallen subsequent to our unit's departure from Pheasy. As for the cots at C 13, we were ignorant of the finer points of field soldiering (and "moonlight requisitioning") and I don't think one cot was smuggled away from the camp.

We stayed in C 13 the next day, spent the next night there, and then the following morning, Wednesday, 22 November 1944, we pulled out for the port of Southampton. There we were split up into various sections and, after much confusion and advice from many parties, we drove our jeeps (mine was with trailer) into the bow of an LST and were lifted up to the main deck on the elevator. We parked and chained our vehicles to the deck. At 2:25 in the afternoon, we shoved off from the not too sunny shores of England. (*In case you're wondering how I remember these details of time, I borrowed Levine's diary for the occasion.*)

It was wonderful to be on an American ship. During our stay at C 13 we had been subjected to C rations, which we found not at all pleasanter than they had been on the 8-day problem at Ritchie, and we were all wondering what sort of a Thanksgiving repast – K or C rations, that is – we were in for. After a few minutes on board the LST, though, and after smelling the odors wafted up from the galley, plus a little "G-2ing" of the crew, we began to have better hopes. Our conditions on the LST, compared at any rate with the Cilicia, were luxurious. We still slept in bunks in three decker arrangement, but they had more space between them, the toilets were more in accord with current fashion in America, and (glory of glories) there were hot fresh-water showers available at all times. (I might add that, if you have never tried to shower in salt water, you have never experienced one of the most frustrating endeavors in the realm of human knowledge.) Moreover, we were not at all disappointed in our expectations as far as the cuisine was concerned. The Navy certainly has the Army outdone by a very long way in that respect. We not only had a very sumptuous Thanksgiving feast, but we were led up to it by some very good meals beforehand. The meals differed in no great respect from the traditional fare – it was just that there were such great quantities and we had not been hopeful of receiving the traditional fare. But it was there: turkey, dressing, mashed potatoes, beans, sweet potatoes, pumpkin pie, all that sort of thing. And the Navy seemed to really enjoy having it for us. The quantities were especially large because about half of our group unfortunately were a little disturbed by the monotonous restlessness of the English Channel and did not care to partake. I, very luckily, was not bothered by such a calamitous misfortune. Because of the attrition, those of us who did eat Thanksgiving dinner were invited to pass through the line as many times as we wanted. And some of us did.

We had to stand guard tours on deck during the two and a half day trip on the Channel, and I can honestly say I didn't mind it a bit. The weather had cleared up considerably; it was warmer, and at night the moon was full, which made a very pretty sight as I sat in the jeep and tried not to be homesick. I was particularly hard hit at that time, because every minute I spent there I kept thinking to myself that my baby might be arriving halfway around the world, and I was powerless to do or even to know anything about it. My guess that he might be at that time in the act of arriving was pretty near right, too, for (as I found out some three weeks later) Jimmy was born on the 24th of November, the day on which, shortly before noon, our LST ground onto the beach in Le Havre, passing up the ruined harbor installations for a clear space of sand. There we unchained our jeeps, hooked up the trailers, and drove them over the ramp onto the beach. We assembled a little while later and started out in convoy for Paris and MIS headquarters in the European Theater of Operations (ETO).

If we had been lucky on our previous convoys, we paid for it on that one. To start off, the convoy commander's jeep turned up with a flat, and we had to wait for him to get that fixed. Then, after conversing rapidly if not very fluently with the first Frenchman we saw (who happened to be a gendarme on duty at the harbor) in order to find out if we could really speak French or not, we headed out on a road that no one knew very well, but which led vaguely east, in which direction lay Paris. We ultimately got there, but not before one jeep had turned over and put its occupants in the hospital (one of them was Buxbaum's cousin) and not before we had traversed probably twice the actual distance from Le Havre to Paris. We drove from noon until six o'clock the next morning, with frequent reconnaissances on the part of the Captain in charge, and infrequent stops for K rations and coffee.

I should explain a little about the rations we received from time to time. The "C" rations were canned meals which we could just open and eat out of the can. The cans contained different meals, some fairly good considering the situation, and some inedible under any circumstances. We had lots of beans in various forms, and stews with meat and potatoes and carrots. All were eaten cold unless there was a convenient fire close by. C rations were standard issue when we were away from a mess where hot food was prepared for the unit we happened to be with. They were not widely appreciated.

"K" rations were supposed to be for emergency uses and were therefore mostly high-energy snacks, candy bars and sweets of different kinds. They were generally liked, and the danger there was to avoid overdosing on sugar. The breakfast K ration was particularly sought after; it was eggs of a sort, mixed with a chopped meat like bacon or ham. Along with their other uses, K rations provided great bartering currency. Particularly the kids were crazy for the candy bars and the chewing gum which was included. They came packed in heavily wax-protected cartons about 9 inches by 5 inches by 3 inches. Most of the time we had a large supply of them stowed in our duffel bags or in the jeep trailer.

"D" rations consisted of single bars of densely packed chocolate. They were designed for real emergency use, something easy to carry in the pocket and gnaw on when it was a long time between meals. I don't believe anyone ever ate a whole D ration at one time; mostly we just gnawed and put it back in our pockets and pulled it out and gnawed some more when we were truly hungry. To the kids of the former German-occupied nations like Holland, D rations were manna from heaven. They would follow us around and beg "kaugummi" (chewing gum) and "schokolade" (chocolate) constantly. After I saw them stand at the clean-up barrel and beg us for the left-overs in our mess-kits, all mixed together, I knew they were really hungry. Obviously, we were incapable of resisting them.

When we ate at other units' messes, the quality of the food varied widely. The same ingredients were used by all of them, but some cooks could do great things with what they had and others tended to slap things together without much concern for quality. Over and over again we had powdered eggs for breakfast. I took an oath that I would never eat anything but a fresh egg ever again. I kept my vow until I had to turn to egg-yellow substitutes in my advanced age. Even there I decided a fresh all-white omelet was better than any yellow-looking packaged product.

The best food resulted from our own group's arrangements after we reached Germany. We always were able to secure a cook if we were going to be at a place very long. We were issued "10 in 1" or "20 in 1" group rations – a ration designed for ten or twenty soldiers. A good cook could work wonders with the ingredients if the basic meat was fit for human consumption. And a really great cook could exchange poor meat for good meat if she knew how to talk to the butcher, as Frau Plöschke was to do later on.

So much for the culinary diversion.

On the way to Paris we went through one town at about eight o'clock at night. I remember the church bells were ringing loudly and everyone was in the streets talking happily. We found out then that Strasbourg had fallen to the French and we got an idea of what it must have been like when liberation was a little bit nearer to home.

We arrived in Paris at around three in the morning. As might be expected, it was quite deserted except for a very few characters who seemed to have nothing better to do than ride around the streets on bicycles at that time of night. I say they must have had nothing better to do, because when we stopped in the Place de la Concorde for a couple of hours while the Captain went to try to find out where MIS headquarters was, several of them stopped and talked to us for a long time. The conversation touched on the black market value of the American dollar and

the British pound, the price of black market cigarettes ($2.50 per pack), the value of nylon stockings in currency or trade, the presence and availability of wine, women and steaks, and other items of interest to the GI visitor to the big city.

Ultimately the Captain returned and we started up again. It was very cold and everyone was very tired. We were hoping very strongly that sooner or later we would arrive at some place where we could lie down in a reasonable facsimile of a bed and get some sleep. Our dreams came true, but not until hours later. We drove from Paris out to St. Germaine, a suburb, and then to Le Vesinet, a suburb of St. Germaine. Le Vesinet was residential but there was a group of buildings that had been formerly occupied by the *Wehrmacht* and which the MIS had just taken over.

When we arrived it was just time for breakfast, so after parking our jeeps in the motor pool we went in and ate what we could of a poorly thrown together breakfast of powdered eggs and coffee. We learned later that day that MIS had just moved to those headquarters from Paris a day or so before and everything was therefore in much confusion, but regardless of whether they had just moved or not, that was one of the most messed-up places I've seen in a long time. I've come to realize this even more as I have seen other outfits move and set up in field conditions in less time than it took that bunch to walk across the street.

Anyway, after breakfast we unloaded our personal stuff from the jeeps and after much discussion about whether we were to stay in this building or that, we were assigned a straw sack, upon which I promptly threw myself and slept until late that afternoon. Most of the others did likewise.

That night I went with Kroner and another boy to see what France was like. We didn't go much farther than a "bistro" a few blocks away, where we talked to the proprietor and his guests, had a red wine or two, and came home again. I discovered that my French, while certainly not perfect, was nevertheless quite sufficient to engage in passable conversations, and I looked forward to really getting it in shape if we stayed there long. The next night we went out again, with the idea of broadening our acquaintance with France, but succeeded once more in getting no farther than St. Germaine, to which we walked (there was a very steep hill and the walking was not much fun) and which we found most uninteresting and already full of soldiers, which spoils any place where you want to talk to people and see what they're like. Accordingly, we did not see too much of France there.

I say MIS headquarters was really quite messed up, and it's really no exaggeration to say I don't believe they had any idea who was there and who wasn't. When I finally found out Sunday, 26 November, that our team was alerted, it was by the purest chance of sitting by somebody at chow who worked in the office and who happened to have a list of alerted teams with him. I don't believe we were ever officially notified. But I found out and discovered also that Murphy's team was going at least as far as the first place with us.

Our team had lost two men in England. Lt. Holmes, who was English anyway, had been sent to the British Army as liaison, and another man, Raubitschek, had gotten chicken pox or something and was in the hospital when we left Pheasy Estates. When we were alerted, we were given a new Lieutenant and a new Tec 5 to bring the team up to strength. The Lieutenant was John W. Walber, a third lieutenant (that is, a Second Lieutenant who had received his commission at Ritchie) and the Tec 5 was Jerry Schaeffer, whom I had known somewhat before, and who seemed to be a very nice man. That made the team consist of Lt. Buxbaum, Lt. Walber, myself, Tec 3 Levine, Tec 3 Schick, and Tec 5 Schaeffer.

At first I didn't care too much for Lt. Buxbaum, and the others on the team positively disliked him. He was very bossy, too exact in his instructions for the performance of every little detail, an inveterate back-seat driver, and generally an old-maidish sort of an officer. He made you very much aware that he

57

was an officer and you an enlisted man. He never neglected to call you by your title, he always gave his commands prefaced by a "Will you please...", but he could at times be cutting and sarcastic and he was at most times very annoying. He came out of it completely (with the exception of an occasional bit of back-seat driving) and developed into a very congenial person. Living and working together in the field and under conditions where we all slept together in the same room and on the same floor brought him down to our level, and he began to sometimes call me "James" instead of "Sergeant Hargrove". He said this in a half-jocular way and I think used my full name to avoid being too familiar and calling me "Jim". I didn't call him "George", but to the EM he was "Uncle George", a term which first was used in sarcasm but which came to be used most of the time almost fondly.

After his "maturity", he stood up for us several times regarding quarters and passes and things, and over time learned a lot about relationships between a CO and his men, especially in a more or less personalized group such as ours. We taught him a great deal, and I claim a large portion of the successful training. I used a device which was pretty effective. I used to write critical comments about him in letters. Sometimes I would get letters from home telling me that he was reading all the things I was saying about him, since he signed as censor. "Fine," I would say to myself. "He needs to know what he's doing wrong." He never mentioned to me any of the comments I made in my letters. As long as they weren't censorable, he learned, kept quiet, and signed the censorship endorsement.

More than once I was the mediator and pacifist between him and the men of this group, although I soon found that I didn't have to do that. The whole history of the team, which started out as a bunch which would get into violent argument at the drop of a hat, was a lesson in human relations, and I think a good one. Uncle George had a healthy respect for my abilities (95% of them relating to typing, report writing and driving) and I always held a favored position with him.

We left Paris about noon on the 27th of November, with the jeeps and the trailer loaded to overflowing, as they have been ever since. Several other teams were going with us to Ninth Army headquarters and we went in a small convoy. The convoy luck which had broken when we hit France continued to break, and this time it was my jeep which was the unfortunate one. In short, we turned over (or half-way over, anyway). I wasn't driving at the time, and if I had I doubt that the accident would have happened, although it was almost unavoidable. Schick was driving. He is none too good a driver, and since the accident was not allowed to drive (not directly as a result of the accident but because he committed the same mistake again after the accident that he did to bring it on).

It had been raining and the road was wet. We were pulling the trailer, and both the jeep and the trailer were heavily overloaded. As we came up a hill and started down the other side, a truck swung out of the line of traffic coming toward us to pass a car, thus blocking our side of the road ahead. Schick jammed on the brakes, which you should not do in the best of circumstances when the road is wet, and with that heavy trailer on back and the momentum of the downhill slant, it was definitely not the correct procedure. The trailer started swerving behind us, skidded on the wet road, and finally pulled us over into a soft shoulder going sideways, which of course turned both the trailer and the jeep over onto our right sides. Having wrecked us, though, the trailer regained its place in our affection by preventing us from going all the way over. I was sitting in the back with duffel bags all around me, and I was so well cushioned I never came close to being bruised. Lt. Walber was sitting in front next to the driver's seat and in the confusion managed to get his shoulder wrenched, although I couldn't figure out how he did it. (Uncle George didn't like Lt. Walber and concocted the story that he had seen Walber put out his right leg to stop the jeep from turning over, hurting his leg as a result. I don't think so.)

Schick wasn't hurt. When we stopped skidding down the hill, we got up, climbed out of the jeep, took inventory and found we had all of our parts, and then looked at the jeep. Most of the oil had drained out, but after we replenished that courtesy of a passing truck, there was nothing organically wrong, so we just turned the jeep right side up, turned the trailer up as well, and went ahead. The only damage was a very wobbly wheel which we later had to replace. Lt. Walber, however, went to the hospital for a week as a result of his shoulder. At least he went there on account of the shoulder; I think he stayed the week on account of the nurses and the food in the hospital.

We drove on until that night, when we stopped in Reims, not far from the huge cathedral, which did not appear to me to be badly damaged by the war. The officers were put up in a hotel downtown, but the poor enlisted men had to sleep in some old French barracks which offered absolutely nothing more than a roof overhead. After the accident, and considering the fact that I didn't get to bed until about 2 in the morning after taking Lt. Walber to the hospital, I did not spend a very comfortable night. Nevertheless, I slept quite soundly and would have slept some few hours more if we hadn't planned to leave at 6:30 the next morning.

22 May 1945
Bad Meinberg, Land Lippe
G E R M A N Y

We were in Reims, weren't we? OK, when we woke up the next morning, 28 November 1944, we discovered that we were too late to get any real breakfast, as they had cooked for only about half the number who were actually in the transit camp there at the time. Accordingly we made the best of a couple of slices of bread and some coffee and prepared to continue our trip toward the Ninth Army.

Our jeep needed some repair work done on one of the wheels, and the trailer wheel was bent badly enough to need a new one, so our team went by the ordnance shop in the town there to have the work done while the rest of the convey pulled out headed for Brussels. The work at the ordnance shop took longer than we anticipated, and it was about noon when we finally left Reims. It was once more a cold and rainy day, and traveling was not at all pleasant in the open jeep. We went up through the eastern route, not passing through any large towns until we hit the Belgian border. I remember we stopped at some small village not far from the border and had a cognac or two plus a cup of bouillon to warm us up, because by that time we were really almost frozen. For lunch we had eaten our K rations with some very delicious French bread, large quantities of which Lt. Buxbaum had acquired from a friend of his living in St. Germaine (he has relatives or friends everywhere, it appears). Shortly before dark we crossed into Belgium, proceeded north through Charleroi, and at about nine entered Brussels.

Besides being tired, hungry, cold and wet, we had driven all day through country that was at best not too beautiful, so when we saw Brussels we were even more pleasantly surprised than we might have been if the trip had been comfortable and interesting. Compared to Brussels, Paris was indeed a dead town. Brussels was definitely alive. The lights burned everywhere, all the movies were open, and there were very large

61

crowds on the streets. The town was at the time in the British zone, and U. S. troops were allowed only on specific orders. Consequently there weren't many of them there. After we made inquiries, we found a restaurant in town which was set up to serve American transit troops, and were once more in for a pleasant surprise. We ate from tables with linen tablecloths and napkins, and from dishes, not mess kits. We were served by waiters, the food was good and there was plenty of it. It was a welcome relief from the K rations motif.

But the best was yet to come. While we finished eating, Lt. Buxbaum went to the phone and rang up another relative of his – the mother of his brother's wife, I believe. She lived in the Rue des Nations at Number 99, her name was Roblin, and she was reputed to be filthy rich. Accordingly we looked forward with great hopes when we went out that way to see about quarters for the night. We were all very apprehensive – after all, we were filthy and disreputable looking, and I think I would have thought twice before I asked anyone looking like us into my house. When we finally located the place, though, we were welcomed with open arms, literally speaking. We all reverently took off our shoes, which were extremely muddy and worse for the wear, and walked in sock-footed. We could have gone barefoot just as well, because there was a big carpet on the floor and it felt like you were walking on a mattress. Mme. Roblin was overjoyed to see Lt. Buxbaum and get some news from her daughter, and she included us in her welcome. We were shown upstairs by her butler, introduced once more to civilized rooms and luxurious beds, and diplomatically led into the bathroom and shown the bathtub. To us at that moment the ultimate in luxury was the oversized bathtub with actual hot water running from the taps.

We lost no time in disrobing and taking advantage of the facilities. I claimed first on the tub and consequently got the hottest and longest bath. We had a contest to see whose water was the dirtiest — Schaeffer and I tied for first, since we had been driving and had gotten the spray from the road. After bathing and shaving we felt much better and were planning on retiring for the night when the butler knocked on the door and informed us he had brought us some refreshment. We went into the bedroom and discovered a tray of champagne, sandwiches, and fresh pears. Considering the cost of these items in Brussels at the time, the small tray was a real treat (a bottle of good champagne cost some 1700 Belgian francs, or about $40, while a loaf of bread was about 500 francs),. As we sipped the champagne and ate the sandwiches and pears we talked to the butler, who was quite a nice chap. We discussed the situation in Belgium in respect to inflation, the German occupation, and the communists. Neither Mme. Roblin nor the butler could speak any English, and so the conversation was entirely in French, which we could all (with the exception of Schaeffer) speak to some extent. Lt. Buxbaum was of course very fluent in French, but he was downstairs talking to Mme. Roblin, so we had no one to rely on. We got along quite well, however.

We spent a very comfortable night in the wonderful beds there. I slept under a fur blanket, which I had never seen before and which I never expect to see again, and woke pretty late the next morning. We had breakfast (toast and jelly and coffee) with Mme. Roblin, and even the meager amount which we had was a strain on her food supply, which at that time in Brussels was very low. After breakfast we once more got into the jeeps, much refreshed and ready once more for the Army. After piling Mme. Roblin, the butler, and the cook with cigarettes and chocolates and taking some pictures (which Mme. Roblin never sent to Lt. Buxbaum), we took off for Maastricht, Holland, and the headquarters of the Ninth U. S. Army.

The drive was better that day. The rain had stopped and the sun was out. The favorable weather and the delightful night we had in Brussels made the prospect quite a bit brighter. We drove east through Louvain, Diest, and Hasselt, and crossed into Holland just west of Maastricht. That was Wednesday, 29 November 1944. We reported to Ninth Army headquarters and came back to Army life with a bang when we were given quarters on the floor of an unused room. We accepted our

63

housing fate for the moment and then went out to see what Maastricht was like. I first hunted out the Red Cross, where I put through an inquiry relative to the baby, hoping to get an answer back in a few days. I didn't hear from the inquiry for about five weeks.

Next day we worked on the jeeps a little bit, cleaning them up and giving them maintenance, and did nothing else in particular. Schick and Levine were assigned temporarily to help in the documents section at headquarters, so Schaeffer and I were separated from them for the night. That day Murphy's team left Ninth Army to go on temporary duty with the 29th Division until our permanent assignments came through. I was wishing we had drawn the assignment so I could have looked up some of Clyde's old acquaintances, but as it turned out they stayed there only one night, so it didn't matter.

That night Jerry Schaeffer and I decided we didn't care about sleeping on the floor in our quarters any more and hinted to a bunch of kids at the garage door that we would sure like some place to spend the night. The Limburgsch dialect which they speak in that part of Holland is very close to German, so we were able to get along pretty well with the kids. Of course when we had made known that we would care to put up somewhere there was an immediate and impromptu battle among the kids to decide who would have the honor. To stop the slaughter we picked one little girl and said, "OK, you're it...where do you live?" She took us around the corner and introduced us to her mother, who was a Belgian and who spoke French as well as German and Dutch. We spoke French to her, and she was so delighted to find an American who spoke French that she was more than glad to have us for the night.

We ate supper at the headquarters mess and returned after supper to sit around and talk to the family. The Van Lith family consisted of a daughter about twenty, a son of eighteen or nineteen and the little girl of about seven who had brought us home, plus, of course, the usual complement of fathers and mothers, one each. All four of the older members of the family spoke French, German and Dutch, and the father and the two older children spoke a little English. Accordingly, through the night the conversation was carried on among various members in one or a mixture of four languages. Mrs. Van Lith spoke French with me because she said she didn't like to speak German. During the evening a GI wandered in who, Mrs. Van Lith confided to me in French, had been coming by every night for about six weeks and just sitting there the major part of the night. As he spoke only English, and as the supply of available English-speakers in their family was somewhat limited, I gathered that he mostly just sat there and looked at the daughter, every once in a while saying "Nice weather, ain't it?" or some other equally brilliant remark. Anyhow, that night we talked until about eleven o'clock, covering the usual subjects, until finally we went upstairs and to sleep in the bed they had allotted us.

Next morning we found out that our permanent assignment had come through and we were to report to the XVI Corps in Tongeren, Belgium (or Tongres, depending on whether you like the Flemish or French spelling), a town about 15 kilometers southeast of Maastricht. Our team, plus another, plus Murphy's team, had been ordered there. Naturally, when Murphy's team got the news, they had to turn right around from Germany, where they had reported to the 29th, and come back to Tongeren.

Tongeren was an old and picturesque town, but not one of the most comfortable or modern in Belgium. Accordingly our quarters were none too good there. When it rained we had to sleep in raincoats to keep the rain which leaked through the roof from washing us away. Then there was the problem with the buzz-bombs (which I never mentioned in my letters home, first because it was prohibited by censorship, and second because the folks at home would have worried, and that wouldn't have helped the situation any).

The buzz-bombs were in fact frequent visitors to our little haven. Most of them were just on the way to Liege and passing over, but some flew a little low, and some even had the audacity

Jim Hargrove

to drop right in town. The day before we arrived in Tongeren one had landed about 500 yards from the EM quarters and had blown out all the windows, which made our stay there somewhat drafty. We were introduced to them in person the first day we arrived. I remember Jerry Schaffer and I were standing by the jeep when we heard one coming over. The putt-putt of its motor sounded like an overgrown outboard motor boat, and we all looked at it as it came overhead. All of a sudden the sound stopped, which meant the motor had cut off, which in turn meant the bomb would come down sometime in the not too distant future and somewhere not too distant from our location.

It was really something to watch the activity when the motor of that thing stopped. The boys in headquarters company had just finished eating and they were standing out in the courtyard washing their messkits. One moment there was a line of some fifty of them standing there talking, some of them watching the buzz-bomb. The next second after the motor stopped there wasn't one of them to be seen, all conversation had ceased, and the space under the trucks in the courtyards was crowded with GIs. I myself squatted down between the jeep and a wall and waited. I looked for Jerry. He had been standing by me just a second ago – now he had disappeared. I looked under the jeep, where I discovered him absolutely flat under the bottom of the vehicle. Now there is not a great deal of space between the floor of a jeep and the street, and I never thought it possible that a human body could make it in one long dive to a prone position under there from a standing position a few feet away. But Jerry did it. The buzz-bomb, incidentally, in case you're still holding your breath, never went off. It must have been a dud.

Not all of them, of course, were duds. I remember one landed in town and blew away a whole block of houses about fifty yards long, killing quite a few and injuring a larger number. At night when you were inside and couldn't see them (you could watch the trail of fire across the sky if you were outside on a clear night) it was particularly full of suspense, because you could never be sure if they were going over or coming in to make a call. At one USO show we attended, several came over during the performance. One came particularly low, and the performer, who was reputed to be a comedian, stopped his act, listened a while and said, "Keep right on going, baby – this ain't home." He got the biggest laugh he had all evening, which tells you something about his regular material. It did keep on going, I'm happy to be able to report.

I remember one other time when we were all in our quarters and we heard a suspicious putt-putt outside. Everybody stopped to listen, but Jerry, who had by that time grown used to them, said "Ah, it's just a truck going down the street." He had no more than gotten the words out of his mouth when a blast shook the building and rattled the windows dangerously near to breaking. There was a moment of silence. "Jerry," someone said, "your truck just exploded down the street!"

Those were the days when Levine slept with his steel helmet on (and a funny sight he was, too, in long underwear and steel helmet crawling between his blankets), and no one cared particularly for the spot next to the windows. For all the damage to nerves and property which they did, though, I don't think there was one military casualty from the buzz-bombs in Tongeren.

So on Friday, 1 December 1944 we reported to XVI Corps headquarters, to which, at least theoretically, we were attached for the duration of the conflict. Life wasn't hard – the officers were quartered in private houses and so had a nice time of it, and although the EM quarters were rotten, the IPW section, with the ingenuity and initiative born of Ritchie, soon secured quarters of their own separate from Headquarters Co. which if not luxurious, nevertheless didn't leak.

The Corps was naturally not in operation, having no troops except those in Corps headquarters, and consequently there were no prisoners to interrogate. We didn't do much of anything – our main problem in life was keeping our jeeps in running order (and, indeed, I think that was always our major problem); otherwise we just sat around, read, wrote occasional letters, and filed status reports to MIS every week with the routine information: "No change in status." Some of the boys were assigned CIC (Counter Intelligence Corps) jobs, which even that early foreshadowed the use to which we would be put following cessation of hostilities.

After a week of such inactivity, we did get a week's break. On 7 December 1944, in order to give us "combat experience" and acquaint us with how IPWs operated in the field, we were sent on detached service to XIII Corps, then in operations in the sector around Geilenkirchen, Germany and south. We left Tongeren about noon and traveled in six-jeep convoy (there were three teams of us) through Maastricht, Velkenberg and Heerlen to the little mining town of Hoenbruck, a few kilometers north of Heerlen, Holland. There we spent that Friday night quartered in a school house that, wonderfully enough, was heated. We slept on the floor, of course, but we were not then acquainted with the finer points of living in the field, and besides it was still Holland, so we behaved ourselves and took what we were given.

The next day we left Hoenbruck fairly early and set out for the divisions to which we were assigned for the week. Our team was sent to the 84th Division, which at the time had its headquarters in Palenberg, Germany. I didn't at the time know Fred Flanagan was in that division, or I would have made some attempt to look him up. We received a cordial welcome from the IPW team then at the division, but were assigned quarters in a very beat-up house. That was not too unusual there because the whole town was pretty much blown to pieces. Palenberg is right across the border inside Germany, and it had suffered the fate of that whole border region. When we entered Germany, the change was so sudden it was amazing. It was as if a line had been drawn along the border and the command given, "Everything east of the line is to be destroyed – nothing west is to be hit." Of course it wasn't that exact, but it was almost. Very few buildings inside Germany were still intact – those that were usually had no roof to speak of. At any rate, the first night we spent in a very dirty, ramshackle and uncomfortable house.

The second day we scouted around and came up with a very well built house which had a pretty complete bottom floor, although it was missing what ordinarily should have been a second story,. We promptly moved in and set up housekeeping. There was a beautiful central furnace which seemed to still be in working order, but when we lit it it started smoking up the whole house, so we set about cleaning it out. The sector was pretty quiet at the time and there were no prisoners the first few days, so we had the time for that sort of thing. We worked on that furnace for the better part of a whole day, and finally got out all of the soot and dust and dirt which had settled in the flue as a result of the bombing and shelling. After that we had a real mansion (or half a mansion) to live in.

Lt. Buxbaum had stayed with the officer of the Division IPW team the first night, but he complained loudly to us the next morning that they had quartered him in a closet (he maintained it was a real closet, no exaggeration). He didn't like the crowded feeling at all, with the cot sticking out into the room where they did the interrogating. The next day he asked us where we had looked for a place, and we told him straight-faced that we had found one that was fine but just wasn't big enough for four of us. That night he moved by himself into the barely standing ruin and tried to sleep on the rushes that had been laid on the floor of the upstairs. The wall was blown off and he had a great view of the outdoors from his sleeping bag. He showed up the next morning, waving his .45 automatic. He was scared to death the whole night, and thought the Germans were going to come after him. He slept with the automatic, although he admitted he kept the safety on.

"That damned house is haunted," he said. "I'd like to move in with you." He obviously thought his comfort and safety were more important than maintaining segregation of officers and EM. We made room for him in the kitchen where I was also staying, and that was where he stayed all during our detached duty. His behavioral training had begun.

Our host team didn't have too much business, so we made little trips up to the regiments, where we met some of the IPW teams who had come over with us. It was their tough luck to be assigned to regimental IPW work while we got the Corps. We visited some of the forward OPs (Observation Posts) and, importantly, learned what equipment and supplies we needed to operate at Divisonal level and what we didn't. In short, we learned the art of living in the field.

Now living in the field at Division is something quite different from living in the field at Company level – as a matter of fact when I say "in the field" when referring to Division duty, I am using a somewhat subtle form of sarcasm which only a real foot soldier can appreciate. The art of living in the field consisted of learning how to start a fire in a coal stove (Mother had given us lessons in the house we had at Blue Ridge Summit, Pennsylvania), how to type with frozen fingers, how to sleep till nine o'clock in the morning and not get found out, how to alter a breakfast K ration so it was good instead of merely nourishing and, above all, how to live with five or six men in one or two rooms without biting each other's head off when the boredom got to you. All these we learned well, although not all on this detached duty trip. And we saw the first indications that Lt. Buxbaum was being successfully educated into the art of human relations, the first lesson of which dealt with the concept that Enlisted Men were not necessarily a lower species than Officers.

At the end of our detached duty, Lt. Walber rejoined us. We once more had our full team of two officers and four enlisted men. Lt. Walber hadn't learned a whole lot of human relations during his stay in the hospital. Several times I thought Uncle George was going to take Walber's shiny lieutenant's bars off and raffle them to the Enlisted Men.

As far as interrogation of prisoners was concerned, the trip was not entirely without worth, although we had very few on which to practice. Lt. Buxbaum interrogated one, and I took my initiation on a half-dead sad-sack of a superman. My German was very stubborn that first time – in spite of all the training and practice at Ritchie, I was scared when I came up against a real PW. Despite the fact that he probably was much more scared and concerned with what was happening than I was, he had no trouble with his native German, and I did with my obviously American version. He had been suffering from dysentery for about two weeks without any medical attention, and he found it very difficult to carry on an uninterrupted conversation. Besides, he didn't know anything worthwhile. Regardless of the negatives, however, I got my first interrogation under my belt, which was, if nothing else, a psychological hurdle I had passed.

After a week with the 84th, we returned to Tongeren and XVI Corps and inactivity. Once more the routine of doing nothing, working on the jeeps, and wishing we had something to occupy our time. But I was greeted on my return with news to banish boredom, at least for a little while. On 14 December 1944 I learned that my son had been born.

The stack of mail was enormous: 48 letters and one cablegram. I disregarded the letters for the time being and ripped open the cable. I had become a father at some indefinite time approximately three weeks ago. Jimmy – despite my previous protests he was named after me as junior – was doing fine, as was Marion. I immediately ran about the place informing all and sundry of the world-shaking news. (I think I even shouted it to Major General Anderson, the Corps commander, as he rode by in his staff car). I was immensely relieved to know everything had turned out all right. All during the past month I had of course been under a big strain waiting for information, wondering if Marion were OK and hoping it was all over without problems. I had tried several times to follow up with the Red Cross, and I had sent a cable home pleading for some word. The information in the cable was sparse, but from its wording and the date on which it was sent I gathered the baby had been born either late on the 23rd or early the 24th of November, just about as I set foot on French soil, as I had speculated.

71

There were other V-mails with further details, some .before Jimmy's birth and some after. None of them mentioned the piloric stenosis which plagued his early months. That was saved for me to know at some later time. It occupied a similar niche as my knowledge of the buzz-bombs.

Shortly after our return to Tongeren, the von Runstedt counter-offensive in Belgium began, soon to be known as "The Bulge". Our first news of the event came when Jerry and I were taking one of the jeeps on a regular trip to Maastricht to the ordnance shop. We were stopped several times before reaching Maastricht and asked for identification, and in Maastricht there were guards posted everywhere. AA positions were all fully manned and look-outs were being strictly maintained. We naturally were curious about the departure from the ordinary, and finally we asked someone we knew what the score was.

He told us that parachutists had been dropped in the area, that some had been caught, but that others were thought to be still at large. This news in the isolated sense in which we first got it, and in the small numbers in which the parachutists had been dropped, didn't make much sense to us at the time. We were to find out later that that the parachutists had been dropped in the wrong area, that they were supposed to have been dropped farther south in sufficient strength to seize important points as the first step of the counter-offensive. The miscarriage of the plans, naturally, did much to prevent the actual success of the initiative. The paratroop plan was so messed up, in fact, that the German Colonel in charge of the airborne operation finally got disgusted, walked into Monschau, and gave himself up.

"I'm disgusted," he was reported to us as saying. "This town was supposed to be in our hands by now. The troops were dropped all wrong and I have no idea where they are now." I could have told him that some of them were up in the Maastricht area, cooling their heels in a PW enclosure.

If the airborne part of the counter-offensive misfired, though, the ground plan seemed for the first few days to be achieving remarkable success. At first we watched the progress of the attack from our seemingly secure position in Tongeren, then as the German penetration grew each day we began wondering if perhaps we would go into operations in a counter-counter-offensive. We were only about 15 kilometers from Liege and reports were drifting through that the German spearheads were seven miles from that important town. Refugees from Liege and other Belgian towns were already streaming through Tongeren. We had to take measures to prevent the refugees from spreading panic – and still we didn't move into line. Divisions after divisions were pulled out of other locations and put into the Ardennes, but our Corps got none of them. Then one night a British unit pulled into town and we were told to pack up. We talked to the Britishers and found out they were supposed to garrison the town, and then we found out that, instead of XVI Corps activating and taking part in the Ardennes battle, we were moving up north into Holland away from the action.

Troops kept pouring through Tongeren, a strict security check was set up, and we had to have darned good identification to walk around the streets after dark. Instead of the standard passwords we were asked things like "Who is Marilyn Monroe's current boyfriend" and "Who catches for the Dodgers", and so forth. The problem was that our foreign-born "specialists" spoke with German accents and didn't follow baseball at all. We put all of our foreign-borns on strict orders never to go out without a native American to go along with them and succeeded in not losing a single one to our own PW cages.

Early in the morning that we left for Heerlen – Friday 22 December 1944 – I stood on the streets of Tongeren and watched a long convoy pull through moving toward The Bulge. I saw by the numbers on the fenders that it was the 75th Division, which our Corps had recently processed and cleared for combat with XVI Corps. I didn't know then, either, that Albert Cowan of Shreveport was in that Division, and he probably sat in one of the trucks that went by me in the street. I found that out later, when I also learned he had taken a bullet through the scrotum which damaged him badly but left him in curable shape, and he was shipped out to warmer climes. The weather in The Bulge was unbelievably cold (below zero Fährenheit for days at a time), and the men on the front lines had to share foxholes to try to avoid freezing to death. The cold weather probably served to minimize Albert's wound, however.

Late that afternoon, after many delays and unnecessary procrastination, XVI Corps headquarters arrived in Heerlen, Holland and began setting up in a large school there. The IPW teams were assigned a room for an office and we were given quarters with Headquarters Company. We weren't supposed to stay there long, but in fact our time in Heerlen was to be some five weeks, during which we met and made good friends with the hospitable Dutch people.

Friday 25 May 1945
Bad Meinberg, Land Lippe
GERMANY

At about 5:30 p.m. on 22 December 1944, we pulled into Heerlen, Holland with the rest of Corps Headquarters, after a very cold and uncomfortable ride in convoy from Tongeren. Heerlen, which was to be our residence for the next five weeks, appeared to be quite a nice town, much more residential, modern and progressive looking than Tongeren, but not as lively or entertainment-rich, not as many shops and commercial establishments.

The first night we were billeted in the building with Corps Headquarters. The next day we were informed that we were moving to another building with some other sections of the rear echelon of headquarters. We moved the following day, which happened to be Sunday and Christmas Eve.

Our set-up in the new building wasn't bad. We found some old beds and with the straw sacks we had picked up for mattresses the place was made fairly comfortable. The building was actually a school no longer used; we slept in one classroom and had our office in another. The building had also been used for a field hospital for nervous cases just before we moved in. The school kids had written notes of welcome on the blackboards, which had never been removed. When we walked in and read "Welcome, heroes, to our classroom! We are praying for a soon recovering", we joked that they had just forgotten to erase the welcome for the nervous cases. If we felt like anything at the moment, it wasn't heroes. We were certainly no fighting troops, we could hardly even consider ourselves in a combat zone, and here we walked into a room with a heroes' welcome staring us in the face!

That night, Christmas Eve, I went to midnight mass in the church in town with Murph (a Catholic, of course) and returned at about one-thirty. The night was clear and cold, the moon was shining very brightly, and we could have thought the world all at peace – if we had not seen the flashes of artillery in the sky ahead and heard the sound of their discharges. Peace on earth was not yet.

Next morning was Christmas, as the next morning after Christmas Eve has been for thousands of years, but it was a pretty cheerless and routine one for us. I went to Protestant services in the church in town and then to dinner at the Corps mess, which was turkey, and which was remarkably good. That afternoon was no different; we sat around and tried to find things to do and couldn't. We read a little bit, and we wished that just one of the bunch had gotten a Christmas package so it would seem a little bit like a festive season. That night we had a small party to try to induce a bit of cheer into the occasion, and on the whole it was successful. The nuns in the convent next door had fixed up some sandwiches from the ingredients we had gotten from the mess sergeant, and they had made quite a fancy arrangement. At least it looked a little like a party. I had a guard tour during most of the party time and consequently missed most of it.

Those guard tours were the worst part of our stay in Heerlen, and the most physical thing we had done since we'd been overseas. Of course there was no real work involved, but it was bitter cold, in the zero range, and standing for two hours was no fun whether or not there was any real exertion. Originally there were other units there at the building and there were enough people to make the tours reasonably few and far between, but after less than a week the other units moved to a different location and we had to stand at least one tour each day. We carried our loaded "grease guns" in view of the continuing battle in Belgium, but our fingers were so cold we couldn't have pulled the trigger, particularly since we wore our specially crafted rabbit-skin mittens which didn't have separated fingers. We would have had to hold our guns with our left hands and pull the trigger with the thumb of our right hands. That we could have hit anything we intended to hit was beyond belief. But we bravely defended the little school in the blisteringly cold night. No one attempted to capture it.

It snowed Christmas Day and continued snowing for several days. Then the weather really got into high gear (or I suppose, with reference to the thermometer, into low) and produced a first class winter – for Eskimos. The native Hollanders kept telling us that it really wasn't supposed to get that cold, that they hadn't had such a winter in a very long time That didn't make it any warmer and consequently didn't help us any.

If the weather was cold, the people in Heerlen were very warm-hearted and friendly. Each one of us had a "family" which adopted him. Some adopted several of us and would have taken the whole bunch if they had just come around.

I met my "family" by unusual circumstances. There were always about a million kids hanging around the building to talk to us, getting a piece of chocolate every now and then, and trying to "kidnap" us and take us home. One day I was standing guard at the gate to the entrance and one of our jeeps came around the corner nearby. Henry Goetz was driving it and just as he swung around the corner one of the little boys ran out in front of the jeep, making it impossible for Henry to miss him. So he hit him, not actually running over him but knocking him down and scaring the daylights out of him. Henry, I think, was more scared than the kid, and he put him in the jeep immediately and took him home and then to an army doctor who looked him over. He wasn't hurt, just bruised. The boy's sister was so scared when she saw the accident (she was standing there at the gate with a whole bunch of others) that she ran home behind the jeep to see what happened to him. Later she came back to tell us he was all right and to ask us over to her house that night. Henry and I accepted, to see how he was doing.

That's how we met the Janssen family. The kid Henry hit was Harrie Janssen, the girl was Diny, and we met the other two children, Niki (four) and Leni (two). Harrie was eleven and Diny fourteen. They were very cute kids, and Mr. and Mrs. Janssen were both very nice. Mr. Janssen was a pretty intelligent man. He spoke very good German They were all so hospitable that we were often embarrassed.   Mrs. Janssen was not particularly good looking, spoke not-so-good German, attempted to steal the conversation from her husband at every opportunity, and was in a condition that made it apparent the family would soon be enlarged beyond the present four children.

The Janssens attached us to the family with a tenacity that was remarkable. Every evening when we left they would insist that we come back the next night, and Diny would absolutely not let us go until we had given our solemn word to return at a specified hour. It was very nice to have someone so interested in you. Although the nightly routine of hearts and "Mensch, Erge Je Niet" (Parchesi to you) got a little boring after a while, we still enjoyed the company and welcomed the opportunity to practice our German.

Jerry Schaffer and I spent New Year's eve at the Janssens, and left shortly after midnight because we both had guard duty later on that night (or morning). Just as we left there was a small scale air attack – the Jerries apparently had decided to help us welcome in the New Year. They dropped a couple of bombs in town, but none came anywhere close to where we were. Lt. Buxbaum did not miss one very far in the place in town where he had gone to a party. The tracers and AA fire aimed at the planes made a fancy display of fireworks to bring the New Year in, and since I don't think anyone was hurt in town, it was all right. The only damage was to the church in the town square where I had gone to Christmas services.

Life continued in its easy-going undisturbed routine in Heerlen for some few weeks more. Most of the time we did nothing except stand the guard tour once or twice a day. One time the Corps Surgeon sent us a lot of German medical magazines (most two to three years old) from which we translated articles dealing with frostbite. We did a pretty good job of it, considering we weren't too familiar with the medical terms. We wrestled over our individual assignments, conferred about the exact interpretation of some of the more obscure words, and only after much sweat and blood arrived at such translations as: "The local phlegmonic infection of the lower tibia could be traced ultimately, then, to the second degree frostbite of the left big toe, the infection having been transmitted through the blood stream and the lymphatic vessels to the point of least resistance in the body." Such a statement in English looks relatively simple, but if you have ever had any acquaintance with medical or philosophical German you will recognize the tremendous potentialities for confusion and circumlocution inherent in such a passage.

After five weeks of pleasant whiling away the time and visiting the *gemütliche Holländer* we received orders to report for temporary duty to V Corps, then engaged in mopping up the erstwhile Belgian Bulge. The duty was supposed to last for approximately eight days, and the orders were cut on 20 January 1945. Not until a long time after did we come to realize the cruel stroke of fate which sheared five points off of our Adjusted Service Ratio Cards (better known as points for discharge). The cruelty was the fact that we left for the Ardennes the day following the date on which the Bulge campaign was later declared to have officially ended, thus depriving us of a battle star for the Ardennes and cutting us out of five more points. Not that I think we should have deserved a battle star if we had left a day earlier; not that I think we deserve a battle star for any of the campaigns we have been in (nobody at Corps or Division headquarters has a real claim to a battle participation star) – but if they had offered me five discharge points, or one, for any reason whatsoever, I would have gladly accepted them.

On 26 January 1945 we pulled out of Heerlen bound for Eupen, Belgium, and V Corps headquarters. The day was extremely cold again, it was snowing, and the wind was pretty vicious in the jeeps. We drove south from Heerlen through Aachen, which was just about five miles or so from Heerlen, then down south farther to Eupen. We were received at V Corps with what I can only call apathy. There was no Corps PW cage, naturally, since no corps ever had one. The V Corps IPW team saw no reason for sending us down to the divisions; and as a consequence we had nothing to do and were considered merely a liability and a bother. We didn't know exactly why we were sent down, but we were given to understand that a large group of PWs was expected and we were to be on hand to assist in the interrogation. Whatever was anticipated, it didn't materialize.

We spent our time either doing nothing or making visits to the various divisions on line, which was interesting and worthwhile to us, but didn't help them at all. Several of the IPW teams in the divisions there were people we had come over with, so we enjoyed the reunion with them and had a good time visiting. The whole time it was unbelievably, intensely cold, and I can't say our quarters were very comfortable, but I must once more remind you that compared to the soldiers doing the fighting we were living in elegance and warmth and comfort. We were, in fact, what the German GI calls *"etappenschweine"*. The nearest counterpart in GI English is "the chairborne army".

While in Eupen we made one side trip to Verviers, which was reputed to be a lively place and a rest center. We enjoyed ourselves, wandering around and buying a couple of souvenirs, even though we found the pickings extremely poor. I sent Marion a very poor quality handkerchief of Belgian lace, which was supposed to be a very high quality item. It was no choice of my own – Jerry Schaffer picked it up when he bought a couple for himself, thinking it would be a nice remembrance of Belgium. I didn't think much of it myself, but after all he offered it to me, and I could hardly bruise his feelings by refusing. Marion was less than enthusiastic about it when she got it in the mail from me.

Lieutenant Buxbaum decided after five days that we had had enough of doing nothing and we could do it just as well back at our own Corps as there, so on 1 February 1945 we packed up everything, piled into our two jeeps, and set out. The weather, glorious to relate, broke that same day, and it was so warm in comparison to the past week that we almost took the top down on the jeep. The wind was still too brisk, though; we changed our minds.

We went back by way of Maastricht so Lieutenant Buxbaum could talk to the MIS liaison officers at Ninth Army Headquarters. While we ate lunch we found out that XVI Corps had moved from Heerlen to Sittard, another Dutch town just a few miles north. We went back through Heerlen anyway to say goodbye to all our friends and find out from the civilians exactly where Corps had moved. If you think I'm kidding, you're wrong. The civilians knew with a great deal more accuracy and with quite a few more details exactly where the Corps had moved and which buildings in Sittard they were occupying.

Later that afternoon we rejoined Corps and found the house which the IPW detachment had taken over as their place of residence. It was comfortable, and after our stay in Eupen and the school building in Heerlen, it seemed almost luxurious. Of course, in comparison with the places in Germany where we later stayed, it certainly wasn't very much. We moved in right after the British left, and the place was more or less a pig sty. They had managed to get things dirtier and more messed up than I would have thought possible. It took us several days to get everything in order.

Up until that time XVI Corps had not been operational, and all the sections in headquarters had been doing the same thing we had been doing, that is, nothing. After about a week in Sittard information came through that the Corps was finally becoming operational, with 35th Division and 8th Armored Division being transferred to XVI Corps in their positions in line along the Roer River front. That meant the headquarters sections had to go to work, although it didn't necessarily mean that the IPWs were going to be much busier for a while, for the front was static and there were only a few isolated PWs being taken. There was no need for us interrogators either at Corps or at the Divisions. But Corps G-2 recognized free labor when they saw it and called on the IPWs to work in their section. Prime requisite: typing ability, English fluency. Chosen: Murphy and me, since nobody else in the outfit typed or spoke English very well.

Murphy drew the day shift, 8 a.m. to 5 p.m. I drew the night shift, 5 p.m. to some unspecified time in the morning, usually between 2 and 3. The work was for the most part interesting and I enjoyed it. I slept late in the morning and didn't get up until time for lunch, which gave me more sleep than I was used to. Moreover, I got in on most of the inside dope. In concert with Murphy, I usually knew more about what was happening and what was going to happen than anybody else around our place. For instance, I saw the order on the beginning of the Roer Campaign almost a week before it came off, and I also saw the proposed site for a bridge across the Rhine after we reached that river. At that time the plans seemed very audacious and I entertained some small doubts that the execution of the assignment would be accomplished with the simplicity with which the order required the "annihilation of the enemy forces west of the Rhine." But shortly over a month after I saw those plans, I crossed that same bridge en route to join the 30th Division.

I forget now exactly what date the Roer Battle started, and Levine didn't have the notation in his diary, but I recall very vividly the artillery barrage which I saw and heard in the distance as I walked home at about three that morning. I was certain then that the static war was no longer static and that events were going to speed up, although I didn't think the end would come as quickly as it did. Mr. Janssen had the turn called pretty well: when I went to tell them goodbye the day we came back from V Corps, he was in a very confident mood. "It'll all be over in three months," he said. V-E Day came nine days later than his guess.

It was very interesting to watch the planned crossing of the Roer River unfold exactly as it was supposed to, even a little faster. I knew XIII Corps, on XVI Corps' right, was to cross first to provide a flanking ground against the extremely strong Siegfried Line defense directly to our front, around the town of

Hilfarth. After XIII Corps had flanked the defenses, our 35th Division was to advance to the river in front of Hilfarth, then run through the XIII Corps sector and attack from the southern flank. 8th Armored Division was to hold on their front along the river farther north until they could cross the river in 35th's breakthrough area to exploit their gains with armor. 79th Division, which had also joined XVI Corps shortly before the attack started, had one regiment, the 314th, on line between the 35th and 8th Armored. It was to act as Corps reserve to be used where and when necessary.

The first few days of the attack I watched the plan progress on the situation map in G-2 at Corps Headquarters. XIII Corps did their job very well; they soon took towns south of Hilfarth and across the river. Then one day we received new orders: we were to report to 35th Division. I knew our sector of the front was about to go into action. On 25 February 1945 we left Sittard and joined the 35th Division at Gangelt, Germany. On 26 February the 35th jumped off, Hilfarth was taken according to plan, and the PWs started coming into the Division cage in batches of 50 and 75. We were finally in action doing the job we were trained to do, and a rough baptism of fire we had, too. No actual fire, of course, but plenty of interrogations in such a rapid succession that we didn't know for a while whether we were coming or going.

The execution of the plan of attack proceeded flawlessly, a new experience for my Army career.

Hilfarth was taken according to plan, and the Heinies were caught somewhat with their proverbial trousers down. We interrogated one German *Leutnant* afterwards. He complained to us in an injured tone that we had done it the only way we could have succeeded. "You had to come from behind," he said. "Our frontal defenses at Hilfarth were too strong for you to breach." He gave me the impression that we had been almost ungentlemanly to run around behind and nip him when he was all set to murder our men when they tried to cross the river.

Jim Hargrove

When Hilfarth fell, the German defenses seemed to melt. They had lost their only good reserve troops in the Ardennes battle, and consequently when we broke through the crust there was no meat in the pie.

Once across the river and through the Siegfried Line, the whole army turned north. One regiment of the 35th climbed on the tanks of a Negro tank battalion and took out on a sight-seeing trip; the next thing we heard of them (the unit was known as Task Force Byrnes) they were in Venlo, Holland, some forty miles or so from Hilfarth. There they took a breather for a few hours, turned east, and headed for the Rhine. They kept going until they met a tight little core of resistance around Wesel, which took quite a long time to liquidate.

The Roer River Plan worked well, the forces west of the Rhine were to a pretty fair degree annihilated, and the *coup de grace* across the Rhine was set up.

1 June 1945
Bad Meinberg, Land Lippe
G e r m a n y

On 25 February 1945 we left Sittard rather late in the afternoon headed for the 35th Div Hq, then located right over the border in Gangelt, Germany. We arrived there about dark and reported in. We were given quarters with the G-2 section of Hq which were none too good, and we were somewhat disappointed that an old outfit like the 35th should not have requisitioned something better. The town was pretty beat up, though, and didn't have much to offer.

That night Lieutenant Buxbaum and I went over and made the acquaintance of the IPW team of the 35th. The team consisted of three men – one lieutenant and two enlisted men. The lieutenant, Ephraim Ackerman by name, was, is and always will be a character of the first degree. He was born in Russia but lived most of his life in Brooklyn. He was about 35 years old, taught Italian literature at NYU, and talked and acted more like a thug than anything else. He won a Silver Star for being the first soldier into a town in France when he entered unarmed under a flag of truce to ask the General in charge to surrender. (P.S. The Germans had pulled out half an hour before.) He had a figure resembling a baby blimp *(this is not a simile invented in my own inactive imagination, but one used to describe my own adolescent physique in the farewell issue of the Purple Pup at Sydney Lanier Junior High School in Houston).*

Besides English, which he spoke very rapidly and without accent except Brooklynese, he spoke some five or six other languages, each as fluently as the other. In a period of two or three days I once saw him interrogate in German, French, Italian, Polish and Russian, and he never had to stop once to think of the word he wanted to use. He had a PhD from NYU, his thesis subject having been "The Economic Factors in the Italian Renaissance". The thesis was rejected twice before he finally argued them into accepting it. Being from Brooklyn, he had a prime case of what George Collier terms "the Brooklyn Psychosis", which means he suffers from a paranoia complex developed in the over-competitive life of that environment. He talked fast and furiously, very rarely finishing a sentence and never allowing you to interject one, always telling you what you were going to say and showing you beforehand that it was a foolish notion. He considered his ideas on any subject the only correct ones and always used an attack as the best means of defending his position.

Well, it was inevitable that Uncle George (Lieutenant Buxbaum, that is) and Ackerman should clash. Ackerman was an old hand at the interrogation game and believed his way was sacred. He interrogated as he conversed, that is, fast and furious, taking things for granted and putting words into the prisoner's mouth sometimes. He seldom knew the composition of the units facing us because he never took the time to find out, and his reports resembled a hasty memo more than a careful document.

When George came down from Corps with an "approved form" for Interrogation Reports, Ackerman laughed at him. "OK," he said, " if the old man wants something pretty to show his friends when they drop in for tea, we'll make our reports in this time-wasting, utterly nonsensical way," He then continued to make his reports the way he always had.

Ackerman ran the show and Uncle George didn't like it, so they weren't too pleased with the situation for the first few days or so. Then they got to know each other, told each other to go to the devil when they felt like it, and did as they individually pleased. After that they got along fine.

I had some trouble with Ackerman at first, too. In the first place, his Brooklyn aggressiveness got me down, and then he tried to get me to make some reports in my own name, which would not only have been pointless but which would have made Lieutenant Buxbaum very mad, and finally he asked me if I didn't want to transfer to his team, which made *me* mad. After a while I got over him, too, though, and learned to ignore his Brooklynisms. After that we all got along fine together.

The last time we saw him was when the Captain and I went to Holland at the close of hostilities. We stopped in at 35th Hq on the way and went up to his room. He was all dressed up in his Eisenhower jacket and overseas cap and was siting in a Napoleon-like pose in front of a camera set up on a tripod in front of him. He had a mirror on a chair and was surveying himself to see that his pose was just right. The camera was set on the automatic release. He was just about to take his own picture. The scene was so typical Buxbaum and I laughed for five minutes. That was his idea of perfection – the perfect cameraman taking a picture of the perfect subject, himself being both.

I have to include an anecdote about Ackerman at this point. It happened shortly after we met him in Gangelt. He decided he needed to instruct us in the way to "break" recalcitrant prisoners – those who refused to give us anything except name, rank and serial number. So he invited Buxbaum and me to his interrogation of a German officer. Now, usually we didn't waste much time with the German officers, because they had tradition and honor to uphold and usually wouldn't say anything. Most of the really proud ones had been taken prisoner and sent to the States with the rest of the Afrika Korps long ago, but a few of the proud ones still remained. Normally we separated the officers and enlisted men as soon as we got them into the PW cage; if they remained together, some of our MPs had forgotten their jobs, because the enlisted men wouldn't talk either as long as the officers were among them.

Ackerman began, as we all usually did, by inquiring as to the PW's army unit and the name of his commander. The officer stood stiffly at attention, gave his name, his rank and his serial number, and refused to speak further. Ackerman blustered around and tried to intimidate him without much success, which embarrassed him in the presence of Buxbaum and myself. So he really got tough.

He told the officer to face the wall, that he was going to count to ten and if he hadn't told us his unit by the time he reached ten he would shoot him. To reinforce the threat he took his .45 automatic from his shoulder holster and put it against the prisoner's neck and began to count. At the count of five he slipped the safety off noisily and jacketed a shell into the breech. The prisoner began to sweat volumes, his legs trembled visibly, and he began to wilt, but he did not say a word. When Ackerman counted the number ten, he moved the gun aside and punched the prisoner in the back of the neck where the gun had been. The prisoner collapsed into an emotional jelly state, thinking for a moment that he had been shot. Ackerman demanded the information again, and this time the prisoner babbled it forth as rapidly as he could. Ackerman said, "Shut up! I already knew what unit you belonged to and everything else about you. Now get out!"

I never saw anyone else do anything like that. It was pure showmanship on Ackerman's part. I was as covered with sweat as the prisoner. I really thought he was going to shoot him.

After spending the first night at Gangelt with the G-2 Section of the 35th, we moved over to the IPW-MP set-up (we usually traveled and quartered together) and Lt. Walber, Levine, and I took up quarters there. Captain Buxbaum, Schick, and Schaffer went over to the Medic Clearing Station to work with them, interviewing wounded prisoners. The next day, 26 February, the 35th jumped off and we started getting our work piled on in earnest. We interrogated until late at night, sweated out our first report until much later, and then climbed into bed to get up at four to move to another CP. That routine was to be regular with us from then until we hit the Rhine.

The next day, the 27th, we moved from Gangelt to Oberbruch, Germany. Oberbruch was just on the west side of the Roer River. When we pulled into the NSDAP (Nazi) headquarters in which we were to be quartered, we found two truckloads of prisoners waiting for us. Not wanting them to feel hurt or left out, we let them help us in cleaning up and blacking out our quarters. We found that a much more satisfactory arrangement than working our own fingers to the bone.

Once we ordered a prisoner to dig a latrine trench for the unit. "It must be just 15 centimeters wide and 2 meters deep! If it is any wider than 15 centimeters, you will suffer the consequences!" we said in our best farcical Nazi style. Of course, it is impossible to dig a trench that deep and only 6 inches wide, but we needed a latrine ditch and we thought it would be amusing to see what he did. In a remarkably short time he announced completion of his task. When we inspected it, it was certainly no more than 6 inches wide. How deep it was we never tried to find out – but it was deep enough. We congratulated him and gave him an extra ration for dinner. He was ecstatic. All the Germans, half starved by this time, thought our food was amazingly good. "Prima!", they would exclaim. We thought the ration was worthy compensation for an amazing latrine trench.

We had pulled into Oberbruch a little before noon. We were set up and interrogating in a short while and kept at it until late that night. Since I was the only one in the team who could type, I wrote most (as a matter of fact all except about two) of the reports the entire time we were working. That meant usually that I stayed up an hour or so longer than the others. I didn't mind it, though, as it helped pass the time quicker and got me tired enough not to think all the time about the long road ahead before we got home. Besides, I was doing something helpful and although in a fast moving situation the PWs seldom have information that is not already out of date, we did pick up some items that added some spice to the routine reports.

As I think back, it seems to me we were longer in Oberbruch than one day, but I can only remember one night spent there, and Phil's diary said only one night, so that's what it must have been. We just did so much during the time we were there that it seemed like a longer time, I guess. We didn't waste much time sleeping.

The next day, 28 February, we pulled out again, crossed the Roer (which is no wider at that spot during normal weather than Buffalo Bayou is where it runs through Memorial Park in Houston) and ended up outside of a little town called Wassenberg, with quarters in an old inn up on top of a hill in the middle of the woods. When we arrived there were seven Heinies waiting around for someone to show up to surrender to. They had been in one of the cement bunkers on the hill and the troops had forgotten them on the first trip through, so they hung around until someone showed up. They came in handy, because once again the rooms needed cleaning up. We stayed there in Wassenberg for two nights, which meant we got a little more sleep than usual the first night.

Very early the morning of 2 March we arose, threw our stuff into the jeeps and trailer, and once more took to the road. Schick had left us the night before for duty with the Medic Clearing Station (the previous Medic detail had returned when we left Gangelt). So there were just the five of us in the two jeeps. That gave us more room than usual, for which we were duly thankful.

The road north from Wassenberg was very crowded and there were traffic jams all the way. Moreover it was very cold, and every time we had to stop for a traffic jam we got out and built fires from whatever happened to be along the road for firewood. In order to get the fire started quickly we would throw a couple of quarts of gas on the wood and stand back. If we had waited to start them in the prescribed manner we would have moved on before they started giving any heat. Further along it got better because when we stopped we would find fires still going which had been started by people at the head of the column.

I remember one time a bunch of MPs, with whom we were traveling as usual, and our team were standing around a fire warming ourselves. The traffic as usual was at a standstill and the convoy had closed up (contrary to regulations) almost bumper to bumper. All of the MPs had their distinguishing helmets on and there was quite a bunch of them there. Suddenly a big sedan with two stars pulled up beside the group, a window rolled down, and General Baade (Commanding General of the 35th) stuck his head out. "Who's the ranking man in that bunch?" he inquired not too politely. Seeing all the MP helmets he naturally assumed we were all MPs. Lt. Walber was standing there innocently warming his feet. When he heard this, he turned around with a satisfied smile looking for Buxbaum. But the Lieutenant had been too smart for him. He had disappeared.

Lt. Walber approached the car like a man approaching a scaffold. "What's the idea of letting the traffic get snarled up like this, and why are all the cars closed up, and what would happen if a Heinie strafed the road now and don't you know the proper interval for cars in convoy and if all you MPs weren't sitting around warming yourselves like nincompoops you'd have this traffic rolling. Now get out there and straighten this traffic out," gently chided the General. He didn't wait for an answer as he told his driver to move on. Lt. Walber's part of the conversation consisted of two salutes and five "Yes, Sir"s, and then he came back to the fire and continued to warm his feet. The MPs thought the term "nincompoops" very funny and laughed a great deal, because they were just in the convoy like everybody else, and they had no idea who was directing the traffic, if indeed anyone was.

Ultimately we arrived at our next CP, which was Kaldenkirchen, quite a ways north of Wassenberg. There we found an even larger number of PWs waiting than previously, and some 30-odd were turned in by the Quartermaster Company, which the boys considered a very amusing situation indeed.

I think it was there that Ackerman demonstrated his technique for handling large groups of PWs. An executive at heart, he usually gave one of his non-coms the job of organizing large groups into their different units. This avoided having to spend time interrogating them individually on this point.

Jim Hargrove

Normally they formed themselves into their German units without incident. This time, however, none of them moved when told to form by units. Ackerman couldn't figure out what was wrong. Then he saw: the officers were scattered among the group of non-coms and common soldiers, and nobody would talk. He blew his top, gave the MPs hell (they loved him) and himself gave the command to organize by units. No one moved. At that he called the MPs over, told them (in English and German, so all the prisoners would know what he was saying) to round up all the officers, take them over behind the barn and shoot them. Then they were to return for further duty.

The MPs complied, separating the officers and marching them off. Just out of sight there was a sudden burst of submachine pistols, a second shorter blast, and then the MPs returned without the officers. Ackerman gave the command to form by units again, and there was a great bustle of activity as everyone hunted for others in his unit. At the conclusion, Ackerman's non-com passed along the line with a clipboard and, with great German precision, the ranking German noncom reported the number of prisoners, ranks and names and units. These were duly entered into the clipboard.

"You see," Ackerman said. "You don't have to always do it the way the book says."

The line of officers came marching back (to separate compounds) as the enlisted personnel watched.

That afternoon word came through for Schaffer to report back to Corps to go to Infantry OCS. I didn't understood why he had applied, and I had told him so several times. We had a much better situation that any lieutenant of infantry would have; why did he want to get involved in the real shooting war just when the end of the road was in sight? But the lure of the shiny bars was too great; Schaffer wanted to be commissioned.

I was selected to take him back to Sittard immediately, then turn around and come back as fast as I could.

Going back to Sittard wasn't hard, although the roads weren't marked yet and it was a pretty good two hour drive, but the return to Kaldenkirchen was quite another matter. Even on my tight time schedule, I ran by Heerlen to say hello to the Janssens (and to eat a family meal for a change). I left Heerlen about dusk, and before I had gone very far it was pitch dark. I had to drive the whole way in full blackout, over unmarked roads pitted with shell holes. And as I drove north into the dark, I remembered that our troops had moved fast and established a long, fairly thin salient. To the left, in Holland, there were still German troops, and so were there in Germany itself, farther to the east. It behooved me to stay in the middle.

At first there was quite a lot of traffic and only one road possible, so I didn't have any trouble. But as the night wore on, the traffic became almost non-existent and instead of a single road there was a complicated network of roads with no markers, either civilian or Army, on them. I exercised my vaunted sense of direction and plowed on north. And of course I got beautifully, completely lost.

The towns between Sittard and 35th Division were completely empty of any troops; in fact they seemed to be utterly devoid of any type of life, civilian, animal or military. I decided that, wherever I was going, I should drive faster so if I got lost I could find myself again quicker and get back to Kaldenkirchen quicker.

The first time I discovered I was lost was quite a shock. I had been traveling along on what I assumed was the right road for quite a while when I entered a very beat up and deserted town. I was curious as to just what town it was, so I stopped and flashed my light around. I picked out a sign which said *"Volledige Vergunning,"* which I took to mean "Fully Licensed". That was all right because it was on a café, but what wasn't quite kosher was that it was in Dutch instead of German. I realized then that I had slipped too far to the west and was somewhere between Venlo and Roermond in Holland. This was precisely where the 35th's advance had penetrated into enemy territory, and one could expect to find pockets of Germans, who might just not be as scared as I was. I hightailed it back the way I had come.

It began to snow. "To hell with the blackout," I murmured to myself, and turned on the full lights of the jeep. Pretty soon I came to another town, equally unidentifiable and equally strange to me. The snow came harder. Then *mirabile dictu*, I saw a U. S. command car at a corner with a couple of GIs in it. I pulled up to ask where we were, but before I could get a word out they shouted, "Can you tell us where in the hell we are?"

I figured they were not going to be any help, but I decided to stick with them for a while because there was a certain comfort in numbers. But then we came to a fork in the road. I recognized one fork I had tried earlier and had been disinclined to continue because of a sign along the edge of the road reading in understandable German, *"Achtung! Minen"* ("Attention! Mines!"). I told the GIs this, but they were not impressed. They determined to try it. I took the other fork. We parted company on our separate ways. I never saw them again.

By devious and doubtful ways, and after many wrong turns of small consequence, I finally found the right road, crossed the pontoon bridge over the little river, and in the early morning hours of the morning discovered home in the form of our quarters at Kaldenkirchen. On a table in the middle of the room was a note held down by a bottle of the Lieutenant's hoarded Scotch whiskey. It said, "We move at four a.m."

We moved next to Venlo, back in Holland. It was only a distance of a few miles, and the main reason we moved was to let Corps move into Kaldenkirchen, which they did a couple of days later. We only stayed in Venlo one night, pulling out on 4 March for Nieukerk, some fifteen or twenty miles east in Germany again. In Nieukerk we stayed in the railroad station in quarters which could have been more comfortable than they were. We had our cots by that time, though, and our quarters were never too bad, only cold. Back in Oberbruch I had "found" a small pot-bellied stove, which we tied on the front of the jeep and took with us everywhere. It gave off pretty good heat, so we weren't really bad off in that respect, either. The only trouble was that my hands were cold most of the time, and it's awfully hard to type with cold hands.

In Nieukerk there were quite a few chickens wandering around without chaperone, and some were in a pen next to the railroad station. We used to watch them intently to see when and where they laid their eggs, but we were unsuccessful in our reconnaissance until one day Buxbaum came in proudly exhibiting one egg, fresh variety, with shell. We all expressed our admiration and pride and asked him how he managed it. "Why, I just went up to one of the hens, pointed my .45 at her, and said, 'Lay, damn you, lay!' and she laid." We all called it rape, but he had an egg and we didn't, so any name-calling was mere spite.

We broke precedent once more by staying in Nieukerk two nights instead of one and getting more sleep than was considered proper. On March 6 it was ordained that the Division had been static long enough and we pulled out that day for Lintfort, some five miles or so west of the Rhine. In Lintfort we set up housekeeping, because the fighting started getting really rough up around Wesel, where the Heinies were making a stand of it, with all their patched-up and makeshift outfits bunched together in a very small area.

Our work there picked up more importance, because whenever a situation began to slow down the G-2 would come running and want to know why, and what the Jerries had there to resist with. Consequently our interrogations, which had become pretty routine, took on added vigor and we started going over the supermen with a fine tooth comb to find out what they knew. One time we had a PW who we knew had information we wanted and who was perfectly willing to give it to us, but who was so dumb we had to work on him some three or four hours to get the details out. That's the worst type to work with, the dumb type. The smart ones who don't want to talk are not nearly so hard; it may take a little time and trouble to break them, but once

95

you have you can get the information in a coherent manner without getting brain fever straightening his story out. Anyhow, we got the information, and so far as the G-2 was concerned, that was all that counted.

We stayed there with the 35th until the Wesel bridgehead was finally eliminated and the division was ready to pull out for a rest and for training in river crossing operations. Then the fate of attached Corps teams struck us again, and instead of being pulled back to rest with the 35th (as the 35th's own IPW team was), we were sent on an assignment to another Division which wasn't resting. It was the 8th Armored Division, the date was 11 March, and the activity was a security check-up, not line duty or PW interrogations.

We packed up, said goodbye to our friends of the 35th, and left that morning for 8th Armd, whose headquarters were in Grefath, Germany. On the way we visited Murph's team at Corps, which was then located in Nieukerk. The IPWs there had a very nice house which seemed very much like a mansion to us after our quarters for the past week or so. And that mansion was in the same town where we had slept in the waiting room of the railroad station! I never did understand why the 35th got such rotten quarters when there were better pickings around for the asking.

In Grefath we joined parts of two other Corps teams and got ourselves a pretty nice house in which I slept on a bed with two feather mattresses. The house had a bathtub with a gas heating arrangement but I never could get it to work properly, so the only bath I took there was a cold one.

Let me describe the bathtub heater: it worked on gas and was fixed to provide only the very minimum amount of hot water possible. It didn't work very well at all on the low gas pressure in the distribution system, which had been badly affected by the acts of war. We found out if we blocked the faucet with our thumbs it would cause the pressure to increase and that would produce lots of hot water. Only you had to be careful not to push your luck too far; if you did, the whole thing was liable to blow up, and you'd have boiling hot water spewing all over you. The trick was to hold it until it was about to blow, then release it and enjoy a cupful of hot water; stop the faucet again and wait for it to almost blow again; and so on until either you got an inch or so of hot water on the bottom of the tub or else you figured it wasn't worth it and you bathed in cold water. Being the conservative one, I always gave up before I got a decent bath.

Our job with the 8th Armd was a unique one. There was a fairly large group of "specialists" and we were assigned to groups of men from the division in a search and interrogation procedure of the whole Corps area.

We worked like this: We would receive our assignment to a certain group one night. The next morning we would join the group in whatever town was to be searched. A cordon was thrown around the town and no one was allowed in or out. Each group was assigned a block of houses, which were entered one at a time. The men from the Division would enter and search while the German-speaking men would gather all the inhabitants into one room and inspect their papers. Anyone without papers or whose identity was questionable would be sent to a screening center for further questioning. The system worked all right except that there weren't enough German-speaking personnel to go around. I was assigned to three groups instead of one, which gave me the job of interrogating the occupants of three houses while they were being searched by each of my three groups. The search was for weapons, ammunition and radio senders, and quite a lot of ammunition was picked up, although weapons had largely already been turned in. A little looting went on, of course, and the main reason more wasn't in evidence was the fact that there wasn't much worth taking.

This I believe was where a German policeman presented me with a 7.62 mm Walther automatic, a beautiful pistol made with the traditional German care and workmanship, and a .25 caliber silver-handled automatic I had in mind for Marion, if she would promise not to shoot me with it. I still have the Walther; the .25 caliber disappeared one day.

The search in the towns was pretty easy, but when we started taking the farm districts and searching across country, the job got a little tougher. One good thing about it was, though, when you found yourself on a prosperous farm about noon time you never had to worry about a meal, and we lived more or less off the fat of the land. Moreover, we of the German-speaking category knew where things were to be had, and consequently during our stay with the 8th Armd we had an abundance of eggs, ham, and once, steaks. I think I averaged about a half dozen eggs a day during my duty there. Of course such provisioning was frowned upon by the authorities, but the people there had plenty (in contrast to the Dutch just a few miles away who had had everything stolen from them when the Germans pulled out), and we paid for what we got, so we overlooked the regulations on the subject.

We stayed with the 8th Armd until 21 March, living comfortably and still working pretty hard and steadily. Bob Beck joined the team 17 March replacing Jerry Schaffer in the Tec 5 position, and thus brought our team up to six men again.

Bob was a native Austrian who had found his way to America, where he joined the Army and was sent to England. He was married; his wife lived in England still. Bob was Jewish, of course, young, energetic, aggressive, inventive, and loved to have a good time. Although he was the last to become a member of our team, he and I did a lot together and became good friends. We were sent home in the same shipment and played checkers constantly on the boat trip home.

Figure 1

257 Langdon Street, Madison, Wisconsin

Figure 2

My "Dutch Family" – the Janssens

Figure 3

My American Family – Marion and Jimmy

Santa Fe Div. Takes 4,000 Prisoners in Rhine Drive

WITH 35TH INF. DIV.—The river-crossing 35th, with a dozen crossings behind it as it stabbed over the Roer River, took more than 4,000 prisoners in the Ninth Army's drive to the Rhine. In 17 days, the Santa Fe division rolled up 30 miles of Siegfried Line, then slashed another 25 miles to crush the remaining Nazi bridgehead across the Rhine from Wesel.

Doughboys of the 320th Regt.'s Third Bn., commanded by Lt. Col. Joseph D. Alexander, of Chicago, mounted tanks to spearhead Task Force Byrne and sped past the Roer's Siegfried defenses to liberate the large Dutch city of Venlo. They conquered Straelen and scores of other German towns, captured hundreds of prisoners by driving almost 50 miles in three days. Climax was a swift night assault on Sevelen.

Lt. Royal Offer of Omaha, Neb., platoon leader of men riding the forward tanks, said: "One of my men had a bullet hole in his left leg and his right leg was almost blown off by an anti-tank shell. Yet he kept shooting. He killed the three soldiers manning the anti-tank gun and forced the officer to surrender."

Task Force Byrne cracked through fierce Nazi resistance and a downpour of enemy artillery to take Drupt.

At the start of the Rhine attack, the 134th crossed the Roer by seizing the stone bridge at Hilfarth. After clearing the Nazis from Hilfarth, the regiment went on to take 20 more towns and link with the British army west of Geldern.

Santa Fe artillery supported the 35th's attack constantly. On one major mission, 13 battalions including corps artillery hit the enemy at once. The division's fire direction center handled three artillery groups and in a single day 11,286 rounds were fired.

Mines were plentiful and the "Brooklyn Beavers" of Lt. Col. Philip Botchin's 60th Engrs. tore through mined steel and log road blocks, filled craters and anti-tank ditches, constructed bridges and effected passage through dozens of enemy demolitions works.

Three 35th Div. MPs not only set up the outfit's PW stockade during the Rhineward offensive, but also supplied the first customers when they nabbed seven Nazis in a courtyard nearby... More firsts: Eight Armd. Div.'s 398th FA Bn. opened the Rhineland softball season when B Btry. trimmed Service Btry., 4-2... Sgt. Huston B. Sweat commands

Jim was there

Figure 4

Stars and Stripes Account of the Roer Campaign

Figure 5

Ninth Army PW Enclosure, Roer Campaign

Figure 6

IPW Team 138
Standing, L to R: Schick, Hargrove, Walber, Buxbaum
Levine, Beck

Figure 7

Beck in the 40 & 8 En Route to Marseilles

Figure 8

Hargrove, bearded and dirty, 40 & 8 to Marseilles

On 21 March we returned to Corps, which had moved then to Lintfort. IPW once more had a beautiful home, once more in a town where we had had uncomfortable quarters when we were there with the 35th. The house we were in with Corps was very large, comfortable, well furnished, and had a wonderful bathroom with real hot water, a luxury which I enjoyed fully, taking baths at frequent intervals of every few hours. Naturally we didn't have anything to do there at Corps, so we spent our time cleaning up the jeeps, getting rid of some of our equipment that we found just got in our way *("Lost in combat", the receipt from the Quartermaster said when Buxbaum dumped all the superfluities – the pyramidal tent still folded in its original configuration, the field desk never used, the camouflage net draped across our jeep hood for effect but never used, and so on)*. We were stripping for the action we knew we would get into when we crossed the Rhine.

There was a very dramatic build-up to the crossing. We could see it coming a long way off, and ultimately could call it down to the day, although since I wasn't working in G-2 at that time, I didn't have the inside picture I had on the crossing of the Roer. We noticed Navy men at mess, handling their mess kits very awkwardly and using Navy slang so that no one could have helped noticing them even if some of them hadn't forgotten to take off the "USN" on their field jackets. Moreover, we saw the huge bridge-building equipment come into the area, and units coming through town with all identification removed from vehicles and men. We knew with confidence that the day wasn't far off. Then when General Eisenhower and Winston Churchill paid our Corps a visit we knew it was only hours away.

On the night of 24 March I went to a picture show there in Lintfort. It was "Till We Meet Again", I remember. I saw it once in Camp Kilmer in the States and have seen it twice more since that day in March, through no fault of my own. When I came out of the theater I saw enormous landing barges moving through Lintfort up to the river. That didn't surprise me very much. At about 2:30 the next morning I was awakened by a very

107

loud and persistent artillery barrage which lit up the sky for miles around and sounded like all the demons in hell being let loose. The artillery was located behind our position, and the shells all passed overhead.

I listened for a while, wished the boys on the river good luck, and went back to sleep.

Next day we received no orders and we began to wonder whether we were going to be in it or not. On the following day, we received them: Join the 30th Infantry Division, which had made the crossing in that sector. Contact them in Friedrichsfeld, on the east side of the Rhine.

The trip in the jeeps across the Rhine was slow, of course, because the traffic across the two new bridges was heavy. Our forces had been getting shell fire on the bridge sites up until that day, but when we crossed it was very quiet and peaceful. The bridge was a rather doubtful looking pontoon affair. It swayed and rose and fell with the heavy current and I had to keep my mind on my job and my eyes on the twin metal strips where I had to hold the wheels of the jeep and the trailer. The river was certainly a different order of magnitude than the Roer, but at that it didn't look as wide as I had dreamed it would be. Slowly we crossed, rising and falling with the current of the great river, and soon set foot successfully on the right bank of the Rhine, on the northern flank of the *Ruhrgebiet* (the Ruhr District) at 12:32 p.m. 26 March 1945. We were pressing against the heartland of the industrial power of the *Dritte Reich*.

We reported to the 30th Div Hq in Friedrichsfeld and were told that the PWE (the PW Enclosure) had moved to a farmhouse some way from the CP, so we set out to find it. On the way I remember seeing a very dead and stiff horse on the side of the road. Most of its entrails were outside of its body, and I recalled the passage in Remarque's "All Quiet on the Western Front" about how horses looked and acted when they died in battle. *There are little scenes like that which stick in your memory for no good reason at all and don't mean a thing but you keep remembering them.*

We found the PWE at the farmhouse and started looking for quarters. The Captain in charge of the 30th's IPW team didn't treat us any too cordially and we had to look for our own place. This was somewhat difficult because there were lots of troops and few farmhouses. We experienced that treatment often, because divisional teams always seemed to resent Corps sending down anyone, but gradually they would get over their complex and welcome us to the magic circle. The 30th was not nearly as well organized in its PW set-up as the 35th, which had devised the excellent system of registering and tabulating PWs by unit. The 30th seemed to go at things in a sort of haphazard blind-folded way. Maybe they didn't do any worse job than the 35th, but it seemed so.

We finally got quarters with the TD Bn attached to the 30th, which was set up in a farmhouse close by. They were very nice to us and there were lots of Louisiana boys in the outfit, so I had quite a few bull sessions with them. They had been with the 30th a long time and had some tall combat stories to tell, particularly about the Ardennes battles, which they had been in up to their necks. They had also seen with their own eyes the American PWs the German 1st Panzer Division had murdered at Malmedy. They hoped fervently that they would run into that outfit some time. I think if they ever had, we would never have gotten any prisoners to interrogate.

The Aid Station of the TD Bn was in the same farmhouse we were in, and for the first time we saw battle casualties arriving with field wounds. There weren't very many, but even the few they had were too many. Most of the time when they brought the wounded in they would report that somebody else in the TD hadn't been as lucky as they, and it would depress the atmosphere quite a bit. The outfit had been together a long time and most of the boys knew each other personally of course. The fact that we all knew the war was in its final stages made it harder for them to reconcile the loss of their buddies.

Despite the fact that the TD Bn had been in combat a long time, they had never witnessed an interrogation of a prisoner, so we brought some prisoners over to the house and interrogated them there. We always had a large and appreciative audience, and when we were through with the important questions we would let them ask questions and interpret for them. Once they asked a prisoner what he thought of our TDs, and when he said he had never heard of them they first got mad and then thought it was funny. "I'll bet your tankers could tell you something about them," they said. But of course there weren't many tanks left in the German army at that time.

On 28 March our team split up on orders from Corps. Half of us, Buxbaum, Schick and I, went back to the 35th, which was located at that time in Dinslaken, some few miles south of where we were. When we got to the 35th, Schick was once more sent to the Medic Clearing Station, which left just Uncle George and me with the 35th itself. We were treated very well by their people. The MPs were very nice and the mess personnel very accommodating in giving me something to eat when I had been interrogating during the regular meal hours.

Dinslaken was very much beat up by the pre-crossing bombardment and artillery barrage, but we managed to find room in the house occupied by the other IPWs and our quarters weren't so bad. Corps Artillery was located all around us, though, and the noise they made sometimes made interrogation difficult. Also, some of the Heinies were still in a shocked condition from battle fatigue and when they heard the guns going off so close they weren't much good for anything.

We stayed in Dinslaken a couple of days and then made a pretty long move east to a group of buildings a little way from the small village of Kirchhellen . We arrived there 30 March 1945 and set up shop in a building which had earlier been a bicycle shop. We had to clear out several whole bicycles and thousands of nuts and bolts to get enough room to set up our cots. During all this time with the 35th Lieutenant Buxbaum and I slept and worked in the same room, which of necessity made the situation a little less formal and contributed to his change from strictly officer to more of a plain co-worker. He also got

110

along fine with the EM in the MPs, so the change wasn't just in relation to me, but in general.

On Good Friday night, Buxbaum and I had settled down to sleep in our room, which was right at the front of the building, when we were awakened by the MP who was standing guard outside. The MP was yelling "Help, somebody, help!" and he sounded pretty desperate. The Lieutenant grabbed his .45 automatic and I grabbed my "grease-gun", the infamous M-3 that jammed about as often as it fired, and we both ran outside in our underwear, the proper sleeping attire for the gentleman of leisure in the ETO.

When we reached the guard we saw he was wrestling with a civilian who was trying to get the guard's gun away from him. The Lieutenant fired high to scare him off, but he didn't scare. We closed in on them and I finally moved around to where I could shoot without hitting the MP. I fired two .45 caliber rounds into his left upper leg. He fell down, which was quite a natural reaction when you receive two slugs of that caliber. What wasn't natural was that he got up again when we started talking to the guard. He walked toward us; we told him to stay where he was but he disregarded us and kept approaching. I fired another couple of rounds wide to dissuade him, and he turned around and started walking away. We ordered him in German to come back, but he didn't pay any attention. I started to fire again, this time for effect, but an MP from the door of the house beat me to it by pumping a couple of shots into him from his .30 caliber carbine.

He lay there as we managed to get a coherent reply from the assaulted MP. He had challenged the man as he approached the bicycle shop but the civilian attacked him and began to wrestle him at that time. That's when the MP called for help and we came charging to the rescue in our underwear. The MP tried to shoot him with his grease-gun, but of course it misfired. That's when we arrived.

By the time his explanation was finished, the civilian had once more gotten up (he had four bullets in him at this time) and

111

started toward us again. One of the MPs who had come out of the house got real irked at him then and shot him in the throat at point blank range with his .45 automatic. The civilian turned a back flip and fell heavily to the ground. We figured then he was out for good and the Lieutenant and I went back inside to warm up and get back to sleep. It was quite cold in our underwear.

As we got back into our cots we heard the noise of another resurrection of the roamer, a startled "I'll be damned! The son of a bitch is still alive!", and another shot of .45 caliber. The civilian then fell down an embankment into about a foot of water. He appeared to be still living, though, and they called the medics and hauled him off to the hospital to try to save him so they could find out what it was all about.

Schick was at the hospital, remember, and he interviewed the man when he recovered enough to talk. He didn't die at the hospital, and Schick said he was likely to recover, but they never found out anything. It was believed that he had suffered a fit or a seizure of some sort and didn't remember a thing about the night. I believed it; no one but a crazy man could have acted the way he did and still live.

That was the only time in my army career that I ever fired my M-3 at anything other than a paper target. I was rather surprised that both the M-3 and I worked the way we were supposed to. The guard was very thankful to Buxbaum and me for "saving his life", because no one knows what the civilian would have done if he had gotten the MP's grease-gun away from him. We comforted ourselves with the thought that it would have misfired again. After that, incidentally, I packed the M-3 away (unloaded), secured a used U. S. Army shoulder holster, and began to carry my 7.65 mm Walther instead. It was much lighter and easier to carry, and I looked real tough in my shoulder holster. It wasn't regulation, but no one, particularly Buxbaum, seemed to care.

Easter arrived on schedule on 1 April 1945. It was as rainy as most of the other days at that time. I went to church at the CP and passed a pretty routine day otherwise. The next day we moved again, to Buer (or more properly Gelsenkirchen-Buer), a pretty good-sized town which had not suffered too much and where we had some excellent quarters in an inn. There was a convenient dining room downstairs, where we ate sitting down at individual tables for four, a nice change from standing up outside and balancing the two parts of the mess kit, the huge tin cup for water or milk or coffee or whatever, and the knife, fork and other necessities. I don't remember using a napkin while eating from the mess kit..

We stayed in Buer a long time, the Division waiting there on the north side of the Rhine-Herne canal before crossing it to participate in the collapse of the Ruhr pocket. During the interval we didn't get many prisoners. What prisoners we did get had swum the canal to surrender to us and were usually half-frozen when they got to us. Considering the fact that we got some fifteen to twenty such deserters a day, it was easy to see that the morale of the German troops in the Ruhr wasn't too high. We did a good piece of work there and knew almost exactly what was waiting for us on the other side of the canal, and where it was. The attack didn't start in our sector, though, and when the 35th crossed there was almost nothing left to oppose them.

Headquarters and IPW crossed the canal on 10 April and took up headquarters in the town of Herne, which had an unbelievable number of civilians running around on the streets. We stayed there several days, once more in an inn, although our accommodations this time were far from the standard of our previous ones. Before we left again for Corps Headquarters, I took the jeep and went down through the bulldozed streets of Essen to Steele. The streets were bulldozed because there was no other way to get through; the bombed rubble of the great industrial city covered everything for several feet, and the Army had brought in the bulldozers to clear the road.

I went to Steele to try to find Norris McGowen, who was with the 79th Division Recon Troop. I found his billet but he was gone for the day. I stayed and visited with some of his buddies, who plied me with a modicum of Norris' scarce liquor ration while I waited, since I was an old friend from Shreveport even though an Enlisted Man. I finally did see Norris for a few minutes but had to leave almost immediately to get back to my IPW team. He asked me where we were and promised to come see me. He also gave me two bottles of his liquor ration. The EM didn't get a liquor ration; every now and then a beer, but nothing else. I thanked him profusely.

Back at Herne, I discovered that Buxbaum had learned, through his own private G-2 sources, of the existence of a *Luftwaffe* (German Air Force) wine and liquor storage facility in a cave not many miles from our location. He said to me, "Now, Sergeant Hargrove, you know those troops guarding that fine wine and spirits will not be able to resist sampling some of the goods. And you know what will happen, don't you? They'll all get drunk and sell the spirits and get caught and court-martialed. We have an obligation to help keep that from happening. I have dispatched a jeep with our trailer to load up with wine and spirits of the finest quality and return them to us for safekeeping. They should be returning any minute!"

He had a point. The troops would certainly get drunk and sell the liquor. And they would have to be punished. We could help them avoid that fate by judicious intervention. But our trailer was already stuffed full of our other paraphernalia. What to do with that? The Captain answered, "We have no additional paraphernalia. It has all been lost in combat. I have filed a combat loss ticket today. The trailer was empty when it left here."

The jeep and trailer returned shortly, modestly packed with wine and liqueurs. The Captain ran gleefully to the trailer, then his demeanor changed completely. "Sergeant Schick," he lectured, "I told you to get only the highest quality product. What you have brought us is quite inferior. It will not do. You must return to the storage cave."

Schick replied that that's all they would give him, and he had to do a lot of talking to get that, he said.

"I shall go back myself," the Lieutenant announced. "and Sergeant Hargrove will drive me."

When we got there, it looked like it was almost too late. It was a very merry group of soldiers guarding the dump, and it didn't look to me that they would be impressed with my leader's disdain for the quality of the goods they had last sent along. I underestimated him. With a few diplomatic remarks and offers of sharing his bounty, he managed to convince them that they really ought to exchange our inferior goods, and they invited him to wander among the stores and select some better stuff. He picked out the very best – the sorts of items that would have been reserved for Hermann Goering and the other generals – and we loaded them to the gunnels of the ¼ ton trailer, whose other contents had been unfortunately lost in combat.

Two days later we received orders to return to Corps Headquarters for reassignment. The 35th was moving out of XVI Corps jurisdiction to resume the chase to the east. We packed up, which was more of a job this time than usual, and were just putting the last of the spirits into the trailer when Norris drove up. "I just came up to have a drink of some of my whiskey," he said. Then he saw the trailer and its contents. He couldn't believe his eyes. "Do you mean this is all yours? All for your little IPW team? And I gave you two bottles of my very own liquor ration? What a traitorous friend you are!"

"Now, Norris," I said. "Let me offer you a couple of bottles of our Courvoisier Napoleon to compensate you for your Scotch. You'll never get any of this in your paltry Officer's Liquor Ration."

He acknowledged this to be true, and he and Buxbaum and I (Schick not participating) enjoyed a round of toasts to mark the occasion. After which he returned to his unit and we continued to pack.

On 14 April 1945 we learned of the death of President Franklin Roosevelt. We hadn't been following the news and didn't know how sick he had been. His death was quite a shock to everybody. Even the German civilians stopped us on the streets to offer us their sympathy. Of course they knew very well by that time who had won the war. They might be beaten, but they weren't stupid.

The return to Corps marked the termination of our IPW work...and the beginning of our new duties in occupation and CIC work. After leaving the 35th Division, we had only two assignments, one to the 79th Division as CIC and one to XVI Corps Artillery, also as CIC.

4 June 1945
Bad Meinberg, Land Lippe
G e r m a n y

When we left the 35th to return to Corps, we did it with many farewells. We were actually very sorry to be leaving, despite the fact that our quarters would probably be much nicer and the work practically nil. Perhaps the last factor was the main reason we hated to be leaving – believe it or not, it is much more pleasant to be working away the time over here than to be sitting around wondering what's going to happen next. Of course for the combat infantryman, I suppose the job is of such a nature that no one really cares about going back to it, but for us the situation was different, and we have always much preferred to be working than loafing.

We didn't exactly loaf when we got back to Corps. Schick and I were assigned to Corps CIC for a few days and the Lieutenant hung around Corps Hq most of the time trying to G-2 the coming situation. Our other half of the team was at the time still with the 75th Division, which was Albert Cowan's outfit, but we were out of touch with them and I couldn't get to them to tell them to look him up. They came back a couple of days later anyhow.

My work with the CIC in Recklinghausen, where the Corps was stationed at the time, had mainly to do with one atrocity case, which Henry Goetz (a member of Murph's team) and I worked on with the aid of a German informer.

The case was one where three English fliers had bailed out of a shot-up plane over Bochum, in the Ruhr some miles south of Recklinghausen. The German who was working with us had been present when the fliers came down. He had been arrested and locked up for trying to interfere when the mob started beating them up. After being severely beaten by the mob, they were shot dead by the local party leader and a couple of others. We worked for three days on the case and talked to about a hundred people in the neighborhood, all except one of whom started out by lying and only told the truth after varying degrees of persuasion. It was here I developed my belief that Germans would really rather lie than tell the truth, because it's easier. Finally we had the satisfaction of arresting one man who had personally shot one of the fliers. The main criminal of the bunch, though, had fled town and was not available. That was the local party leader. We also arrested a couple of people who admitted to beating the fliers with rakes.

Right after we wound up that case we received orders to report to Lüdinghausen, a town about 25 miles northeast of Recklinghausen, for duty with a branch CIC detachment from the 79th Division. Although the CIC unit was from the 79th, the troops in the area (except for Norris' 79th Recon Troop) were all from the 18th AAA Group. It was there that Lieutenant Buxbaum received notice of his promotion to Captain, long overdue, certainly in his mind, and I happily received my elevation to Master Sergeant as well. We celebrated together.

At Lüdinghausen we had what was and probably will continue to be the best set-up we've had since we arrived in England. We stayed in a house with a Military Government detachment. The CIC consisted of five EM and two officers and the MG detachment had five EM and three officers. With the one officer and two enlisted men in our half-team, we had a very comfortable household for our mansion. We drew our rations from the AAA outfit and had our separate mess, under the supervision of a fabulous creature we all called "Frau Plöschke", although that wasn't her name and I don't know what her name really was. She did the cooking and lorded it over the two maids who did the cleaning up and washing and sewing. She was a veritable fiend when it came to food. She cooked fantastic amounts and insisted that we eat it all. She never let a coffee cup get more than half-empty. She asked twenty times during a meal whether we thought it was any good or not, and she got her feelings hurt if we didn't each individually answer her each time in the most superlatively affirmative phrases.

One day we received in our rations some pork chops which we were supposed to have for dinner. They were really very inferior pork chops – 95 % fat and the residue sickly looking low-quality pork. She came immediately to the Captain: "Herr Hauptman," she said, "the pork chops are not very good at all."

"Yes, I can see that," Buxbaum replied, "but that's what we got and that's what we'll have to have."

"But, Herr Hauptman, they are really very poor pork chops."

"There's nothing I can do about it."

"But they are all fatty…"

"Frau Plöschke, we will have the pork chops for supper. That's all."

She retreated to the kitchen, muttering to herself with every step, "But the pork chops really aren't any good at all."

Later that day, unknown to us, she marched down to the local butcher with a package under her arm. She stalked (all 200 pounds of her) into the shop and nailed the butcher with an eye that must have outdone the one with which the Ancient Mariner buttonholed the wedding guest that day.

"Herr Schneider," she said, "The Germans need more fat in their diet."

"Agreed," acquiesced the rather puzzled butcher.

"Herr Schneider," she continued relentlessly, "I have here some very nice pork chops with an amazing abundance of fat. They would be good for the deficient German diet. In return I want only that insignificant little beef roast" [it weighed 15 pounds if it weighed an ounce] "which you have reserved for the Landrat."   [The Landrat was the equivalent of a district governmental commissioner in our terms.]

"But, Gnädige Frau…" the butcher began.

"Herr Schneider," she interjected, "it is for the American Gestapo, for whom I am the chef. They would regard your agreement as a token of good will." And she must have made some sort of significant gesture at that point, because the butcher quickly consummated the deal and ushered her out of the shop.

That night the Landrat ate some very fatty pork chops and we dined in state upon a beautiful beef roast cooked very deliciously. That was the night Charlie Roberts and I got in about 9:30 from the day's rounds and she stayed there and heated up the roast for us again and served it to us – and told us the story of her visit to the butcher, with much laughter.

Yes, Frau Plöschke was quite an admirable housekeeper – and chef.

If the set-up was magnificent there, though, we worked hard enough to earn it. We arrived on 17 April and from the next day until the day we left we went out every morning at 8:30 and got back about 7:30 or so in the evening on average. We covered from 50 to 60 miles per day visiting all the little towns under our supervision.

The set-up was this: In our CIC work, Lt. Conyers, from the 79th CIC, organized the detachment and stayed in town to take care of local matters with Captain Buxbaum. Then there was a British sergeant in the equivalent of their CIC who stayed in Lüdinghausen taking care of the jail and any incidentals to come up. The other four men were divided into two teams: Charlie Roberts, another British sergeant, and I were on one team and Herb Schick and the remaining Britisher made up the other. Why the Britishers? Because ultimately the territory we were working was to be included in the British zone, or so we surmised.

Charlie and I worked one half of the *Kreis* (equivalent to a U. S. county) and Herb and his partner the other. Charlie was a very nice fellow and we got along fine together. He didn't speak any German and so I did the lion's share of the interrogating, while he talked to MG (Military Government) officers and discussed the subjects with me. I never could understand what good it did to have CIC men who didn't speak German – they could do very little except office work and advisory functions – but he was good company and it was nice to have the responsibility divided when we had to make decisions, sometimes hard ones.

I suppose you have a pretty good idea of what CIC work is, but I'll give you a general picture of it anyway, without going into the details of how we worked.

In general, our mission was to arrest all Nazis (members of the *Nationalsozialistische Deutsche Arbeiter Partei – NSDAP*) over certain grades in the Party, to prevent or break up subversive activities, and to remove all Nazis from public office. The latter job was by far the hardest, because all public officials over here for the past twelve years have been obliged to be members of the Party, regardless of how long they had previously been in government. We therefore had to use some common sense in that phase of activities in order to leave the MG officers someone who knew a little bit about governmental administration. The part about subversive activities was not very important, because we never ran into any concrete instances of resistance, and most of our work in that respect consisted of exploding rumors.

I was practically Czar of several little towns in my area. With our mission and with the power which we had to throw people in jail without normal judicial protection, it is understandable that we were feared, respected and rigorously obeyed wherever we went. The German penchant for obeying authority enabled them to accept the new Allied authority and discard the old Nazi one without demurral.

With the 7.65 mm Walther in my shoulder holster or slung around my hips like a cowboy, I was enough to scare all the governmental people we dealt with. When we came to a town, the *Bürgermeister* would rush out of conferences on food supply, sanitation, or whatever else was at hand, closet himself with us, and give instructions he was not to be disturbed on any account. Orders, requests, demands, or other communications from Allied officers as high as Majors were swept aside if we asked for information, or a list, or anything else. The attitude is understandable considering what the word *Gestapo* meant to the Germans for so many years. High party officials or high army officers were as nothing compared to the simple Gestapo representative, and although we studiously avoided any comparison of ourselves to the Gestapo the comparison was nevertheless drawn, despite the fact that we were not secret and were always uniformed.

The respect tendered us, incidentally, did not stop with the Germans. We could walk into any troop command post and receive an immediate invitation to dinner; we were presented with all kinds of problems from the handling of DPs (Displaced Persons) to the restoration of water supplies, and we were treated with consideration by officers who would under normal conditions probably never even have noticed us. The acronym "CIC" carried some magic connotation with it, and I believe most of the hurried, overworked, non-German-speaking officers with whom we talked believed we carried a crystal bowl around with us into which we could gaze and make unerring decisions on any point at a moment's notice. When they asked us to "screen" public officials (which, meaning "investigate for political reliability", was part of our job), they thought we could talk to a man for five minutes and pass inerrant judgment on him. Of course, we could find out as much of his background as he wanted to tell us in that time, but real investigation took longer, talking to other people in town, etc. Moreover, when we recommended dismissal of public officials they would ask us whom they should put in their places, which was *not* a part of our job, but before we got through we would frequently have to hunt around to find a suitable replacement.

CIC work (at least the work we did) is not, however, a "cloak and dagger" counter-spy activity, as press releases and a certain article in the May 1945 issue of Reader's Digest would lead one to believe. Furthermore, in its present state of flux and change, it is not highly efficient and consists of a combination of luck and technique and persistence. The luck is probably the largest element. I remember when we picked up the murderer of the English flier, we went by his house in the rather vain hope we might find some clue as to his whereabouts. He was actually in the house himself at the time, having returned a half-hour earlier to get some of his clothes. By that stroke of luck we gained a large reputation among the people in the vicinity, who did not know that it was pure luck and assumed we had a large number of undercover agents in the area. We didn't tell them otherwise.

Considering the position in which a CIC investigator found himself, and its various advantages, you might assume that I enjoyed the work. I didn't. I dislike arresting people. Even if I know for sure that a man is a thoroughly despicable character and deserves to be arrested, I can't enjoy taking him away from a family and locking him up. I did it, of course, because that was my job and I thought it was a necessary one, but I didn't enjoy it.

The German attitude toward arrest was very peculiar. Very few people — even very few wives — put up a fuss or tore their hair or made other demonstrations. They accepted it apathetically and seemed more or less to expect it. I suppose that is one indication that the arrest is justified, if the man and the family accept it as natural. Unjustified arrests, incidentally, are among the things we have most to guard against. It is a favorite trick of the Germans to air a personal grievance by bringing some vague and unsubstantiated charge against a personal enemy, and it is up to us to prove or disprove the charge. When we find out that the charge was untrue and based purely on personal grievances we usually give the plaintiff a quiet little talking-to and scare the daylights out of him, in order to remind him of the ninth commandment.

We stayed in Lüdinghausen from 17 April to about 5 May, when the area changed hands and we were ordered to Corps Artillery to join the other half of our team, which had been assigned there shortly after we left for the 79th. At Ludighausen, incidentally, was the 79th Recon Troop, and that meant Norris McGowen was there. I saw him several times, although not nearly as much as I would have liked because I was gone all day and when I came home at night I either had reports to write or I wanted to write a letter or two.

123

We arrived in Bad Salzuflen, Land Lippe, Germany, on 6 May 1945, having spent one night at Corps in Bochum, where Murphy's team was still holding down the unenviable Corps team assignment. Land Lippe is a very pretty spot, almost completely untouched by the war because it was a hospital district for the *Luftwaffe*. Even now, in Bad Meinberg, there are several large hospitals. There are also PW Enclosures in the park in the center of town.

In Bad Salzuflen we worked with Corps Artillery in much the same capacity as with the 79th in Lüdinghausen, that is, as CIC, although the set-up wasn't as good and the system not well organized when we first got there. In due time that changed, and the only thing wrong after that was that we had only breakfast in our house instead of all three meals.

From Bad Salzuflen Schick and I worked the territory for a while, then that territory was assigned to someone else and we started working another. I had the beautiful little undamaged town of Lemgo for a while by myself. It is an old (16th Century) picturesque town, where much still exists as it must have done for many years, embodying all the good things of Germany now largely destroyed. It is a town that radiates *Gemütlichkeit* and *Brudershaft* and after the war it became a favorite tourist target.

In Lemgo, at 3:00 p.m. on 8 May 1945, I interrupted a conference with the Police Chief to listen to an announcement over the Chief's small radio, which was connected to the public address system around the *Rathaus* square. The sonorous, powerfully dramatic voice of Winston Churchill boomed over the square as his historic address to the House of Commons in London was broadcast: "German armed forces surrendered unconditionally on May 7…Hostilities will end officially at one minute after midnight to-night (Tuesday, May 8) but in the interest of saving lives the "Cease Fire" began yesterday to be sounded all along the front…" At this point suddenly the great bells of *Sankt Nicolai Kirche* began to toll, followed by all the bells of the town. Cheers began which continued uninterrupted for a very long time.

124

The Germans were not cheering the surrender of their country's armed forces. They were cheering the final cessation of a brutal, long-endured war of enormous proportions. They were acknowledging their defeat at the hands of vastly more powerful opponents who also happened to have the cause of justice on their side, and they were sounding a reveille for a new beginning. It was very moving.

The War in Europe was over.

We stayed in Bad Salzuflen only a few days, leaving there on the 11th for Bad Meinberg, some 20 miles south, which is where we have been ever since. We have a better house here than we had in Bad Salzuflen, we have two maids to fix breakfast and clean up, we sleep on beds with sheets which are changed every three days, and in general we live very nicely. We worked pretty hard for the first two weeks, after which the flux and change of war caught up with us and we were told to cut our operations and bring our files up to date. We stopped operations altogether except in emergency cases, and right now we are in the process of sitting around and waiting to be relieved, which might be tomorrow and might be next week – or some unknown time in the future.

What will happen when we are relieved is a question which, at last reports, remains unanswered. We receive comforting bulletins from FID (Field Interrogation Division of MIS) every now and then which inform us that they don't know anything about the future, and then we hear the latest rumor as to what XVI Corps Headquarters is going to do, sympathizing or rejoicing with the men in response to the current reports. Three days ago I could have said with a fair amount of assurance what was in store for Headquarters, but today the situation is very muddled by scores of conflicting rumors, and I would hesitate even to say that tomorrow will be Tuesday.

A day after we moved to Bad Meinberg the Captain came hurriedly into my room. "Quick, Sergeant Hargrove, come with me. We are going on a little trip."

125

I began to ask a question and he interrupted me. "Later. In the jeep. I'll tell you all about it."

He had received a visitor, not identified to me, who told him that a man who was Major-Domo to Joseph Goebbels for years was located a little to the north of where we were and wanted to tell his story to an American Counter-Intelligence team. We were going to meet him and bring him back to Bad Meinberg.

"Why all the secrecy?" I asked

"Because he's in the British Zone and they'll steal the story from us if they hear about him," the Captain replied. I knew this was probably true; there was a good bit of competition between the two services. We were at the northern extremity of the U. S. Zone; the British Zone was just a few miles away.

We reached the boundary, waved cheerfully at the lone British soldier on guard there, and proceeded to the little town of Bueckeburg, southwest of Hannover. Buxbaum had the address, which we found easily, and in a very short time we had Wilhelm Rohrssen in the jeep with us. Our return through the British Zone back to Bad Meinberg was easy and uneventful. What we had done was counter to all the regulations about working with the British in our area. But we had scored a coup.

We interrogated Rohrssen for three days. Buxbaum did most of the questioning (although all we had to do was just let him talk) and I took copious notes, translating from Rohrssen's German into English as I scribbled madly on the pad of paper. From time to time I would ask questions for clarification and in order to slow down the rapid pace of the monologue. After we had gotten everything he had, we took him back to Bueckeburg.

I held out a copy of the Rohrssen interrogation for my own file. It was classified, and I didn't write Marion or anyone else anything about it at the time. Now my copy of the interrogation, retyped recently, is included as Appendix A-1 to these letters.

The story was very interesting. There was always the question of truthfulness, but we resolved that in Rohrssen's favor because it fit most of what we already knew about the last days of Nazism in the doomed city of Berlin. The report, signed of

126

course by Buxbaum, was sent up through channels to the Corps G-2. As far as I know, neither Buxbaum nor I heard any more about it ever. But once a few years before this writing, Marion and I were watching a television program entitled "The Last Days of Berlin". As the story developed, both of us realized at the same time what it was: the script of the program followed very closely parts of my report on Rohrssen. I got my copy of the report and followed it on the screen. The report was not copyrighted. I had no claim to title. I let it go. I still read it again from time to time.

Incidentally, the tomb of Frederick the Great, where Rohrssen speculated that Hitler's body had been secreted, was opened later. Hitler's body was not there. The story of his cremation outside the bunker is the presently accepted version of the Nazi Göttedämmerung.

One week after the Rohrssen interview, Captain Buxbaum and I made a short trip to Heerlen, Holland, to pick up the footlockers which he and Lt. Walber had left there when we pulled our for Divisional duty. We stayed a day and a half, which was very pleasant, but it was a long drive and not too easy. The *autobahn* was in pretty good shape, but many of the overpasses were still down and we had to exit and re-enter often. From Dortmund on, and especially over the Rhine, the roads had been beat up very badly by all the traffic and they were full of holes, so riding over them was somewhat like riding over a magnified washboard. We took fifty eggs along with us to the folks in Heerlen. When we got there about a dozen were broken from the rough ride, but they were not so completely smashed as Humpty-Dumpty and were still good enough for scrambling. The Janssens were delighted with the eggs, but the younger kids wouldn't eat them, never having tasted them before.

The Janssens were very glad to see me and I was enthusiastically received. When I started emptying my musette bag of the chocolates I had been saving for the last three months, my welcome turned almost into a mob scene, and Niki and Leni started leaping around and yelling "Santa Claus" or its equivalent in Dutch. Leni ate three bars before her mother noticed how she was gorging on it. Her mother was too interested in the ten bars of soap I brought her to notice much of anything. Besides the chocolate and soap I brought Mr. Janssen some cigarettes and pipe tobacco. Cigarettes are selling in the black market there now for 6 guilden, or about $2.25, while farther north in the newly liberated districts they are about 8 ½ guilden a pack. I don't think I would ever want a cigarette bad enough to pay that for them.

I didn't do much there in Heerlen. The first night I just sat around with the Janssens and talked. Mr. Janssen said the war with Japan wouldn't last more than six months. The next day I went downtown and spent some time getting a barber shave, some time in the Red Cross Club, and some in the public bath, where the showers were as hot and comfortable as ever. That afternoon I drove Captain Buxbaum to Maastricht, where we did nothing much in particular, and I came back and went to see "Daar Kommt Mynheer Jordan" ("There Comes Mr. Jordan") at the local cinema. The next day I took a couple of rolls of pictures of the Janssens and the new baby because they can't get any film in Holland. I left one roll with them and one I brought with me and had developed in Bad Meinberg. The pictures turned out very well. I sent the first prints to the Janssens.

Next day Captain Buxbaum and I made the long ride back, this time through Köln and Paderbord. The road was better.

After we got back we didn't do much of anything except wait around for orders. The most work I did was to grease the jeeps and paint out the "XVI – IPW 138" on our bumpers and repaint them with "MIS – ETO" in anticipation of our next move.

I did stir from my lethargy to take a walk with Bob Beck out in the country. We were searching primarily for some horses to ride, because the country is so pretty, and we felt in the mood for it. We did finally find some, but the owner only had one saddle. We took turns riding him. His name was "Prince".

I discovered that European horses don't respond to the same reins guidance as our horses, and consequently when I first mounted Prince and went through all the motions of setting the beast in motion, nothing happened. The horses weren't well trained, even to European commands, and it wasn't much fun. I found out that what Ernie Pyle had to say about Italian mules in "Brave Men" was true, that is, one says "Brrrr" to an Italian mule to make it go. This seems to hold for German horses as well. The only problem is you tell it "Brrrr" not only to start it but "Brrrr" to make it stop, back up, turn to the right or left, lie down, play dead, jump a fence or do anything at all. If you just say "Brrrr" long enough, they go through their whole routine.

That brings me up to date. I am sitting in a little office in the former home of Dr. Freericks (who conveniently died a peaceful death some months ago), the time is 2115, and the date is 4 June 1945. The little pond behind the house is once more placid after having been disturbed earlier by the natives swimming in it. The sun is setting slowly behind the hill where Corps Artillery Headquarters are set up in a former maternity home (it stays light until about 2230 this time of year). And I am slowly going nuts wondering what I will be writing in another recapitulation six months hence.

Would that I could write the future as easily as I can remember the past!

Jim Hargrove

In der Heimat, in der Heimat,

Da gibt's ein Wiederseh'n

[In the homeland, in the homeland, there'll be a Wiedersehen -
German Folk Song]

Jim Hargrove

Augsburg, Land Bayern
16 June 1945
G e r m a n y

Augsburg is a pleasant city, an old, undamaged town where it is very obvious that one is in the *gemütlich* environment of Bavaria rather than the vigorous energy of the *Ruhrgebiet*. Here one enjoys some of the best German beer and actually sees men wearing *lederhosen* (short leather pants) and hears them talking in a *Schwäbisch* dialect that makes it difficult for even our native-German-speakers to understand them.

But the *gemütlichkeit* is lost on IPW Team 138. We are back in the army, and we don't particularly like it.

We received our orders finally and packed up to leave Bad Meinberg immediately. Early the following morning we left in a convoy of two jeeps, the leading one (driven by me, since Schick was disbarred from the steering wheel position) pulling a ¼ ton trailer filled to the gills with a great deal of personal paraphernalia and spirits (mostly liqueurs and cognacs, since we had drunk up most of our *Wehrmacht* wine); and only the smallest modicum of Government Issue impedimenta. We headed due south, toward Seventh Army Headquarters at Augsburg, through the countryside of Westfallen, whence comes the best ham in Germany, the famous ham that is to be eaten raw, like Italy's *prosciutto*, except *Westfällischerschinken* is eaten in raw chunks rather than in the paper-thin slices of *prosciutto*. We were in a hurry so we didn't stop to pick up a supply to take with us.

We drove through a high divide, I believe a part of the *Harzgebirge*, a remote, rugged looking landscape that reminded me of the divide west of Kerrville in Texas. Then we detoured, turning somewhat westerly, proceeding through Hessen and stopping for the night at the little resort town of Bad Schwalbach outside of Wiesbaden. This put us some 15 miles east of the Rhine River just below the rocks of the *Lorelei* (I recalled, silently for the benefit of my co-passengers, the *Lorelei* song they had taught us at Madison: *"Ich weiss nicht was soll es bedeuten, Dass Ich so traurig bin. Ein Mädchen aus uralten Zeiten, Dass kommt mir nicht aus dem Sinn"*). But we didn't have time to visit the famous *mädchen.*

We had stopped at Bad Schwalbach because it was the Headquarters of MIS, of which we were a field unit. The Captain hoped to get some indication of what we were going to be doing in our new assignment, and how we could improve it. He was always working at improvement – of assignments, of quarters, of amenities of all sorts. The Enlisted Men left him to do his G-2ing and looked around at the old, quiet, aristocratic baths, band shells for evening concerts, gambling houses. MIS was very good at selecting elegant headquarters sites, and Bad Schwalbach was no exception.

I believed Jess Bessinger was or had recently been at Bad Schwalbach, and I looked around to see if I could find him. He had been reassigned from his Photo Interpretation work at Patton's Army Headquarters and was supposed to be in prospect of redeployment. I hadn't looked long before I heard him – that commanding operatic-strength voice – and soon he appeared. We had a great reunion. He was in his tale-spinning mood and had many a wild and probably hyperbolic tale to tell me. I don't think I got a word in edgewise. He had the definite advantage, having been close to Patton much of the time. And much of what I could have told him I thought it better not to talk about, like the interview with Rohrssen. So we had a few beers, reminisced, talked of home, and shot the bull. Then he told me he was to be redeployed very shortly: Paris, the States, and then the CBI (China-Burma-India Theatre). I envied him the stay in the States, but I wasn't too anxious to head for Western China. I doubted they would have much use for my German experience, though, so it was academic.

The next morning we continued our trip south, the Captain having learned nothing worthwhile during his stop. Through Wiesbaden we drove around Frankfurt-am-Main to the autobahn toward Karlsruhe. Before we reached the west-east autobahn toward Stuttgart and Augsburg, we left it in order to take local roads to see some of the scenery.

As our two-jeep *cum* trailer convoy was passing through the small town of Ettlingen, a rather portly middle-aged woman ran out into the street in front of us, waving her hands wildly and risking life and limb as she shouted something in German. We screeched to a halt and the Captain tried to calm her down and find out what was wrong. She said she was trying to continue operation of her family's champagne winery, her men having long ago gone off to war. She had been assigned a Russian prisoner to help her run it, and he had become very aggressive since the end of the war. Today he had gotten quite drunk off the champagne (or *Sekt*, the German equivalent) and was chasing her around the house with all sorts of threats and erotic intentions, she said. And he was breaking bottles of the precious *Sekt*. At this the Captain leaped into action, recognizing the value of a continuing supply of champagne. He ran into the house, corralled the offender, his .45 automatic in his hand, and lectured him severely in his native Russian. Then he brought him out of the house, deposited him in his jeep, and announced he would get rid of the troublemaker for the *gnädige Frau* by depositing him in the local DP (Displaced Persons) Camp. She was ecstatic, and announced that she would like to give our group something for our help. The Captain detailed several of us to go into the winery and see what the lady had in mind.

What she had in mind was about a third of the supply of *Sekt* in bottles on the racks. We rearranged the already full trailer and loaded the newly-made space with bottles of champagne. From that time on, when we would run out of the sparkling wine temporarily, a jeep would be dispatched to the winery again and the trailer replenished. We were never without champagne after that, often drinking it in the early evenings because our paltry beer ration of two cans a week had to be saved for more auspicious occasions. To say that it was equal to the best produce of the Champagne country in France, centered on

135

Reims, would be a stretch, but it was certainly adequate for our untutored palates, and the Captain graciously put up with it.

After the *Sekt* incident we proceeded (without sampling the product) to the ancient and historic city of Augsburg, founded by the Emperor Augustus, and the site, some 1500 years after its founding, of Luther's *Augsburg Confession* during the Protestant Reformation. We shrugged off the impressive history of the city and reported to Seventh Army Headquarters in an old German *Wehrmacht* Training Camp.

Culture shock! Seventh Army was a spit-and-polish outfit; we were a bunch of independent "specialists". At Seventh Army the Enlisted Men were quartered in a big, open, bare barracks with wooden bedstands and straw sacks (straw sacks! memories of Glasgow!) for mattresses. Latrine facilities matched the décor of the bedroom, far down the line from the sleek new (if Spartan) facilities I was greeted with in basic training at Camp Wallace. We agreed that it was hard to get back to the Army after so long an absence fighting the war. There were "gigs" for not wearing a tie (we hadn't had one on since they took them away from us at Pheasy), a curfew for EM at 9 p.m. (by which time we would probably be asleep anyway, admittedly), and a "Post Theatre" instead of just a "movie house."

It was generally agreed that our stay at Seventh Army had to be a short, temporary one, after which maybe we could resume our old *personas*.

Aalen, Bayern
23 June 1945
G e r m a n y

Aalen is a big improvement over Seventh Army Hq in Augsburg, especially insofar as our quarters and other items of ambiance are concerned. We have been sent as an attached unit to 12th Armored Division, whose mission is to discharge a substantial portion of the German Army, keeping only those who can be identified as NSDAP functionaries, personnel of the *Sicherheitsdienst, Gestapo, Schützstaffel – Waffen SS*, and any others questionable from a political point of view. The men in the 12th Armored don't have the slightest idea who is or who is not in these categories; we are supposed to screen them all and tell them which ones to send to an internment camp and which ones to throw back into civilian life to provide food for the winter and to rebuild the rubble of the *Dritte Reich*.

Our quota is to discharge some seven thousand men in an average day. We work from six o'clock in the morning to about five in the afternoon. If we take only 10 seconds each man to screen them, we can do about six a minute, or 360 an hour, or 3600 in a day, taking some time out to eat. That's per interviewer. With four active interviewers per team, that would mean 14,400 per team, or twice our quota of seven thousand a day. So we could take as much as 20 seconds per interview.

But 10 or even 20 seconds a man is hardly enough to ask for the soldier's "*Soldbuch*", a record of his service and his pay intervals, and ask a question after looking through it. It's ludicrous to think we can ferret out possible subversives in that time, or it would be except for the propensity of most of them to answer correctly when they are asked, "Were you ever in the SS, the SD, the Gestapo, or the NSDAP?" Frequently they will nod and admit that they were. Of course it depends on which service they were in. If they were minor members of NSDAP, they will tend to admit it, and if they were in the *Waffen SS* (the military units of the SS), they will admit to that also, since many of that

137

service were simply drafted into it. If they have a background in the higher ranks of the Party, the SD, the civilian or Waffen SS, or the Gestapo, they will evade or lie about it. It is, of course, impossible to really mask membership in the SS: they all bear their SS serial numbers tattooed permanently on the underside of their left arms high up just below the shoulder.

The little fish will usually admit their antecedents. The really big fish will lie over and over again attempting to avoid them. We can usually find out in a short time, but not within the 20 second limit we need to observe to meet our quota. We point out to the 12th Armored people that probably a number of the bigger fish are slipping through and returning home free men, which doesn't seem like such a good idea. The official word is, "Don't worry about losing them; they'll get picked up when they get home anyway." We don't believe it.

The ones we tag for detention are hauled off to an internment camp (we try to avoid the use of "concentration camp", which has some unpleasant connotations) where they will be interviewed again, sometimes several times. Such a camp is located not far from Aalen, near the village of Kornwestheim, a suburb of Stuttgart to the south and Ludwigsburg, a noble city with a beautiful castle, to the north. We presume that's where our rejects are to be taken.

The accelerated pace of intense interrogation takes a toll on our people. I am probably less impacted than most of the others on our team, because I don't have as much of the deep-seated fury and resentment as Jews have at the ways in which their people have been brutalized and killed by the Nazis. My Jewish compatriots hate to miss someone who deserves to be punished for his part in the holocaust. And so do I; but I don't have the intensity of their *angst*.

Of course, the army has a valid purpose in the frantic discharge of the German army. The agricultural production season is hard upon us, and the rich fields of the German breadbasket need to be tilled and planted and harvested to avoid mass starvation in a country as ruined as Germany has been, and where there is no possibility of importation from those countries which they have ravished for years. If we are not to be faced with feeding Germany during the coming winter, we have to turn loose their workers.

And so we do – at the rate of seven thousand a day in our center alone.

We returned to self-sufficiency when we were detached from Seventh Army Headquarters and sent to 12th Armored. The latter unit didn't want to have to fool with us and so suggested we find our own housing and make our own arrangements through MIS for our rations. We chortled inwardly as we professed dismay outwardly. Within an hour we had a lovely two-story house on a quiet, tree-lined street looking toward the Kocher River and the high hills to the east beyond. We hired two maids to work full time for us, and we each had a separate room (not a separate bath, though) and a comfortable living and dining area.

We had escaped once more from the octopus-like tentacles of Army entrapment.

Jim Hargrove

Aalen, Bayern
15 July 1945
G e r m a n y

Excerpt from a letter written from Aalen this date:

I shall tell you tonight of the story of my visit to Dachau Concentration Camp, located just north and a little west of München (Munich). The story has a beginning a long way back. I suppose to really reach its origins we would have to go back about 34 years to the time when Herb Schick, the Tec3 on my team, was born in New York City.

His parents were Austrian Jews who had moved to America in the early part of the 20th Century. Not long after Herb was born they were called back to Vienna by the serious illness of his grandmother. After they got back, his grandmother lingered longer than had been expected, and as a consequence their stay in Austria was prolonged. After his grandmother's death, there were business affairs which kept them there even longer. Then, in 1914, World War I broke out and his father, still an Austrian citizen, was drafted into the Austrian Army.

The relevance of all this to my visit to Dachau may be obscure at this point, but I want to establish the facts that Herb Schick was an American citizen by virtue of his birth in New York City, but that he grew up in Vienna and lived there almost all of his life.

Ten years after Herb was born, the Schicks had another boy, this one born in Vienna, an Austrian citizen. He was named Otto. These were the only children in the family. Time passed as it always will, and years became decades until finally the time came that Adolf Hitler engineered the *Anschlüss* that made Austria an appendage of the *Dritte Reich.* This had a profound influence on the Schick family, as on all the Jews in Austria and elsewhere in Europe.

One day the Gestapo walked into the Schick home in Vienna and walked out with the elder brother, Herb. After a little

140

preliminary questioning in Vienna, during which the only pertinent fact was that he was Jewish, he was loaded into a special train and, along with quite a few others, shipped off to Dachau. He stayed there for about four months, after which he was transferred to Buchenwald, which was a change of scenery but otherwise, in respect to the treatment he received, all the worse.

All the time he had been gone, the Schicks in Vienna (his father had died and it was just his mother, his brother, and some other relatives) were conferring with the American consul about his case. As he was an American citizen by birth, the American Consulate was ultimately, in December of 1938, able to negotiate his release on condition that he leave immediately for the United States, alone, without his mother and Otto Schick or any other relatives. There was also the matter of paying for an exit permit, a normal requirement for the release of Jews.

The day before he left he married, although he had to leave without his wife as well; she was an Austrian citizen. After he reached the States (he could speak no English, having to learn it from scratch), he immediately began to negotiate to bring his wife and mother and brother over as well. Ultimately he succeeded in bringing his mother and his wife, but not his brother. He was making some progress, but it was slow, and he had been unable to bring Otto over by the time war broke out between the United States and Germany in 1941. Then it was hopeless.

So Herb had parted from his 10-year younger brother in 1938 and hadn't seen him since that time. In the States they heard from him of course until the war, and after that they heard no more except once indirectly from relatives that he was hiding in Hungary from the Gestapo. After that rather discouraging bit of news, there had been no word at all.

When Herb came to Europe in the U. S. Army, he made inquiries as to whether he could get in touch with anyone in Vienna, but he had not been able to do so. He had always been very concerned about his brother's whereabouts.

That was the story until three days ago.

A Captain who is attached to Headquarters of 12th Armored Division came into the room where we were screening PWs. He said to Herb without preamble: "Schick, your brother is a guide in Dachau, where he was found when the Americans took the camp two months ago."

Of course Herb was flabbergasted and asked where he got his information, but it was very vague, and there was nothing definite. An officer from the G-2 Section of 7th Army, the Captain said, had gone through Dachau and had been conducted on the tour by a boy named Otto Schick, who said his brother was Herbert Schick and that he was in the American Army. The officer from 7th Army happened to know where he was. Army passed the information down to Corps, which passed it down to Division, where it finally got to Schick.

The next day Captain Buxbaum, Schick and I made the short trip along the autobahn to the München area. On the way we stopped at 7th Army Headquarters to see if there was any mail for the team. Surprisingly, there was, the first that we had had since the first part of June before we left Bad Meinberg.

Among the other mail was a letter for Schick – from his mother, who had received a letter from Otto and was writing to give him the information. She had tried to cable, but our mail was so messed up it never got to Schick. Her information was likewise vague. Otto was in the hospital and the letter was written and mailed by an obliging U. S. soldier. It merely said he was suffering from typhus fever and weighed only 90 pounds (Otto is as tall as I am). He was recovering and would be all right. The letter was written in May.

We proceeded to Dachau. We inquired in the administration building and found out he was indeed in the camp and working as a guide at the main gate. We went over to the gate but he was not there. We inquired from another guide where he was. The other guide looked at Herb and asked, "Are you Herbert Schick?"

Schick acknowledged that he was. The guide rushed over to the car, shook hands vigorously and cried, "Oh, I am so glad. I am Otto's best friend. Come, I will show you where he is!"

We all piled into the jeep and he led us over to the road toward the Crematorium. There was a bunch of British soldiers touring, and a boy in the blue uniform of a camp guide. Our guide jumped from the jeep and yelled, "Otto! Otto! *Hier ist dein Bruder! Dein Bruder ist hier!"* ("Here is your brother! Your brother is here!")

Otto looked hard, located him in the front seat, and ran over to him, sobbing, "Herbert, oh, Herbert!" while the British soldiers, the Captain and I looked on. The drama, the emotion of the moment were overwhelming, the two of them embracing there after an absence of seven years when they didn't know whether the other was alive or tortured or what.

Of course, it was only by a series of close calls and a large amount of good luck (or providential care, as you wish) that Otto was still alive. When we saw him he had already put on weight since the letter to his mother. He still looked pretty bad, very gaunt, and the marks of the typhus were still on his face.

Since Herb had left Vienna, Otto had been hounded from pillar to post. He had been arrested once and escaped just before his group was shipped to Russia as forced labor. He had then hidden out in Hungary for a long while and finally was recaptured. Since his recapture he had been in more concentration camps than he liked to think about. He named five of them to us; of them all, Dachau was one of the easiest, he said.

If Dachau was easy in comparison, the others cannot be described.

At one of them they had forced the prisoners to build a hangar out of cement, carrying big blocks of cement by hand from four in the morning to ten at night, with only the meagerest of rations. After that camp, he said, they were loaded onto a cattle car train for transport to Dachau. On the way, they had to pass an ammunition train stopped on a stretch of rail because of bomb damage to the tracks. American planes were overhead.

The train commander had stopped it right next to the ammunition train, which was helpless before the attacking planes. They attacked, of course, and ultimately set the ammunition train on fire. In the explosions which followed, the transport train was set on fire, too. There were seventeen cars on the transport train. Fifteen of them burned up. In each car were 125 people (they were of the French "40 & 8" type, designed for 40 men maximum). As the cars burned, the occupants were burned to death or trampled to death by others trying to get out. If they succeeded in getting out they were gunned down by the train guards. They pulled the transport into Dachau with all of the corpses still in the smoking cars.

Otto was in one of the two cars which did not burn.

In Dachau, they were informed by the prisoner foremen that they had been brought there for liquidation. They would be sent to the gas chambers the day after next. The evening of the next day, however, American troops stormed Dachau, surprising the SS guards and capturing the camp intact. There were about 2,000 SS guards in Dachau. No prisoners were taken; no guard was left alive in Dachau that night.

Otto had come into Dachau with typhus, and the first night in the camp he ran a very high temperature (when he was admitted to a hospital the Americans set up there, it was 104°). He hid his condition, telling no one about it. If he had told the guards, he would have been sent to the "hospital" whose two rooms were located adjacent to the gas chambers. No one ever got well from the "hospital". After American hospitalization and a good diet, he recovered. Now he looks fine.

He eats ravenously every chance he gets, and he will probably be overweight in a short time. He loves American music, especially "Don't Fence Me In," which has become his theme song in constant performance, despite the fact that he has no aptitude for melody that I can discern.

We left Herb and Otto together and went to inspect the camp. Otto's Hungarian friend showed us around. I know you have all read the stories of the gas chambers and the crematoria at the concentration camps. I had read them too. But there is something about the very idea that makes one refuse to believe it could really be as bad as it was described. When I saw the place I had such a feeling of disgust I don't think I could ever describe it. It wasn't that it was filthy or frightful looking. On the contrary; most of the evidences of the murders had been removed, and the place was clinically clean. It was its very cleanliness and order that raised the level of my disgust and incredibility. It looked cold, commonplace, businesslike, Germanically efficient. It was a human slaughterhouse, and death there must have been looked upon with all the indifference and apathy that surrounds the death of cattle in a cattle slaughterhouse.

On the walls of the crematorium itself were the words, *"Reinlichkeit ist die erste Pflicht, Deswegen muss sich jeder die Hände waschen"* — "Cleanliness is the first duty, therefore everyone must wash his hands." The irony of it on the walls of the furnace, the ultimate symbol of filthy murder, was too great. Aside from the gas chamber, where there were facilities for gassing some hundred and fifty persons in one room simultaneously, there were as many other methods of killing people as I could think of, all of them so barefaced and open that it took your breath away. There's no point in going into them all. It was terrible.

The story is amazing and horrible, but it had a happy ending for Herb and Otto. Today Lt. Walber and Herb and Bob Beck went back to Dachau and got Otto's discharge papers from the camp. Otto ate dinner with us here tonight. He seems to be a very nice young man. He has rooms at a home here in Aalen. Herb is going to see what can be done about taking him back to the States when he goes himself. In the meantime he has become an adjunct member of IPW Team 138.

145

Otto gave me some *"Kragenspiegel"*, collar patches or insignia, which had the stylized initials "SA" and "SS" on them – for *Sturmabteilung*, the SA that the Horst Wessel Song sings about: *"Die Fahne hoch! Die Reihen fest geschlossen! SA marschiert; kommt Ihr, marschieren mit!"* The SS Guards at Dachau were part of an elite group of SS troops, SA of SS who carried the *Führer*-awarded title of *Leibstandarte Adolf Hitler* – Adolf Hitler's Bodyguard. Otto had picked up a number of the *Kragenspiegel* as souvenirs.

Aalen, Bayern
23 July 1945
G e r m a n y

Excerpt from a letter of this date:

The Captain had put through a request for leave to go to Prague to search for some of his relatives from whom he had not heard since before the War. The request had been pending for more than ten days, with a discouraging prognosis and no further word of any kind. He was getting more and more nervous about making the trip. The reunion of the Schick brothers intensified his compulsion to seek out the survivors of his own family. A few days ago he came to me and asked, "Sergeant Hargrove, I am about to leave for a trip to Prague. Do you want to go with me?"

"Sure I do, Captain," I came back quickly. "Have you gotten your leave, then?"

"No," he said. "I'm going VOCG." Now VOCG means Verbal Orders of the Commanding General. I knew enough about the situation to know that meant the same thing as going without orders. Travel beyond the American occupation zone in Czechoslovakia meant crossing into the Russian territory, and American trips of that kind were strongly discouraged. We would need a special pass to cross the demarcation line, which we would have to secure from the Commanding General of XXII Corps, occupying our zone in Czechoslovakia. His headquarters were at Pilsen, in Czechoslovakia. The Captain had never met him, and of course neither had I.

It sounded like a great opportunity. I said something similar to Ruth's pledge to Naomi: "Whither thou goest, I shall go..." but I stopped at the part about "where you die, there shall I die, and there shall I be buried." That seemed a little unnecessary. The Russians were our convivial wartime allies, weren't they?

The trip was a little long in an open jeep and over the wartime roads. Our biggest problem was a supply of gasoline.

147

Jim Hargrove

We filled three extra Jerry cans and piled them into the back of the jeep. I wondered how long they would last on the streets of Prague.

It didn't take us nearly as long to get to Pilsen as I had thought. Of course, we didn't take the time to visit Bayreuth, although we went right by it. Anyhow, the Wagnerian festival wasn't being done this summer.

Buxbaum was in XXII Corps Headquarters over four hours. He finally managed to get an appointment with the Chief of Staff and put his case poignantly and forcefully (I know because he told me) until finally the C of S threw his hands up in surrender and ordered a pass for him and his driver (me). Although by this time it was late in the afternoon, we headed straight for Prague, not too far distant from Pilsen in miles but a long way in terms of security. Our passes were very impressive, written in English, Czechoslovakian and Russian and stamped four times with the official XXII Corps stamp.

We crossed the Demarcation Line with very little trouble because of the pass and an ample supply of cigarettes, which we had had the foresight to take along. The Russian method of challenging, incidentally, was to demand, *"Papiri, Papirosi!"* or something like that. *"Papiri"* meant our identity and pass cards, and *"Papirosi"* meant cigarettes. We responded to the challenge by presenting the pass and cigarettes together, at which gesture the Russians accepted the cigarettes with broad grins, shouted *"Tovaritsch"* a couple of times, neglected to glance at the pass at all, and waved us by.

There were only a few Russian troops in the area, and what there were looked more like creatures from the *Grapes of Wrath* than formidable modern soldiers. I heard later in Prague that most of the good Russian troops had been withdrawn and only a scattering of inferior units were left.

We soon made our first acquaintance with the Russian transportation system. It was really quite simple and remarkably efficient, not to say cheap. Anyone traveling in a certain direction merely walks up to a road block, waits till a car comes

148

going his way, hops in with a grin, a "*Tovaritsch*", and a word I took to mean "Thanks" when he got his cigarette. At the second road block we picked up (or were picked up by) a Russian lieutenant and his girl friend in the established manner. He was going only a few miles up the road but the girl was going all the way into Prague. The Captain talked to her in Russian and learned that she had been born in Paris of Hungarian parents but had been brought up some place in the Ural Mountains of Russia. She was serving in some vague way with the Russian Army, the nature of her assignment seeming to elude exact translation. She was very helpful, though. Whenever we came to a Russian road block afterwards, she would stand up in the back of the jeep, wave furiously at the soldiers on the road block, and shout in Russian: "Let 'em by; let 'em by." And they let us by, saving both time and cigarettes. When we pulled into Prague we let her off at the hotel where she was staying. She obligingly informed us of the number of her hotel room, which we acknowledged and promptly forgot. We weren't interested, and besides her knees were very dirty.

In Prague we pulled up confidently at the Hotel Alcron and the Captain went inside to arrange for rooms while I stayed out with the jeep, which we were given to understand would disappear at a moment's notice if left unguarded on the streets. In a few moments the Captain came out again with the information that there were no rooms available and we went off to another hotel. The story was the same, and we were told there that we would have to apply at some governmental building for a room reservation. We proceeded to the place designated, and the Captain went inside and talked for some two hours to various and sundry people in various and sundry departments, ultimately coming out with some very official looking document and a reservation at the Palace Hotel, where we stayed for the three nights of our pass. We unloaded the full gasoline cans and locked them in a closet. We chained and padlocked the steering wheel of the jeep and took the distributor cap with us to our room. We always removed it when we left the jeep for any time, no matter where we were. We didn't want to lose that jeep. Our room was fairly nice for the Prague hotels of the time, I suppose, although it wasn't too large, with the bathroom about twice the size of the room itself.

After we got settled in the hotel we went over to the Hotel Alcron again to eat supper. We were introduced to the protocol for military personnel eating without food coupons. It was very simple. A young lady was stationed at the door to the dining room, and when we came up she handed us two food coupons. We took two steps inside the door and handed the coupons to the waiter and all was accomplished. Simplicity itself.

The meal was even simpler. There were four courses, just to maintain the reputation of the hotel, but all four together wouldn't have made the equivalent of the peanut butter and jelly sandwiches we used to eat at Madison before retiring. I doubt that the enforced diet hurt me in the least. I don't know, however, how the people there live off of that menu day in and day out.

After dinner we took a walk around the town and visited several of the coffee houses for which Prague used to be famous. Of course there was no coffee, so they served a liquid known as "Limonade", which could be any one of six differed colors but which always tasted the same, like water with perhaps a pinch of cherry jello flavoring added. It was cool, anyway, and wet, and we drank several glasses of it. It was an exciting drink – there was a great deal of suspense involved in waiting to see what color our "Limonade" was going to be.

We got to bed about twelve that night and slept very soundly in our room, which was very hot but nevertheless very comfortable after the long drive.

The next day we had a better look at Prague. It was really a beautiful city, basically undamaged from the war, a combination of the old world and the modern, of narrow little alleys and broad avenues, old architecture and new, counterpointed artistically in a way that reminded me of Mexico City. I think it is the prettiest city I have yet seen in Europe. The government

150

buildings on the hill overlooking the Mulda River were especially striking. They were all in one area, with the huge castle built by Holy Roman Emperor Carl IV some six hundred years ago dominating the group. President Benes was then in residence in the castle. Right in the middle of all the government buildings is the magnificent Gothic style Church of St. Vait.

In the middle of all the old stately government buildings there is a sleek polished marble obelisk that looks very much out of place. We found out that it was put there by the Germans to commemorate some unknown event. The Czechs hadn't got rid of it yet, but I am confident they will if they have to use dynamite. They are deGermanifying the country with remarkable vigor.

Most of the first day in Prague the Captain spent looking up members of his family and friends whom he had last heard from in 1939. He was signally unsuccessful. He found one cousin who had returned with his life (and nothing else) from Theresienstadt, Ausschwitz and several other concentration camps. From him Buxbaum found out "all the bad news of the last six years, condensed into two days." None of the rest of his family, including a numerous bunch of cousins, had returned from the concentration camps to which they had been sent. Whatever else the Germans might have failed to accomplish in Czechoslovakia, they succeeded in very efficiently disposing of about 90 per cent of the considerable Jewish population there.

That night we went with the Captain's cousin, whose name was Weinmann, out to his house and had dinner with him and his wife and his four year old daughter. His wife, not being Jewish, hadn't been sent away. We had a very nice dinner, much better than what we got at the hotel, and a pleasant evening sitting around and talking. I had to speak French with his wife as she didn't speak English. I hauled it out of its dark recess and dusted it off and gave it a game try. But every time I started to say something in French it came out in German.

The next day we slept a little late but got over to the Alcron again for breakfast at about nine. Same breakfast: bread and

151

coffee. We had taken some of our own coffee, though, so it wasn't bad. When we pulled some cigarettes out of our pockets and laid them on the table, the headwaiter began to take a special interest in us and we ended up with some salami to go with the rolls.

The Captain then attended to some other business connected with a factory his father had owned in Upice. He found that it had been taken over by a worker's committee and was being operated on a soviet basis, with all the incidents of ownership going to the workers. Buxbaum wanted to come to Upice to see for himself, but the manager to whom Buxbaum was speaking spoke strongly against it and said he couldn't guarantee his safety. Buxbaum reluctantly stayed away. I was sorry for him, but I was in the jeep, too, and I didn't like the "no guarantee of safety" comment.

We went shopping with Weinmann along to show us where to go. There wasn't much to buy, and the only thing I got was a silver pin with the Czechoslovakian emblem on it. It wasn't much, but even at that I had to dig up some silver Dutch coins I had been saving for six months, in order to compensate the artisan for the silver in the pin. We later bought some lithographs of scenes in Prague, mostly on the Charles Bridge, which I sent home.

At one point we went by the American Embassy and talked with Mr. Perry, the consul. He was very pleasant, with a good sense of humor. We talked about an hour. Later we went to the house of a friend of Weinmann's for tea (salami sandwiches) and then to Weinmann's home again for the rest of the evening. Mrs. Weinmann was learning English and I tried to help her with that while in turn learning a little Czechoslovakian. I came away with the idea that the language was like none I had any familiarity with. I contented myself with "Please" and "Thank You" and I tried to learn how to say "Three", which is "Tri" in Czech and ought to be easy. But there's a little "v" over the "r" in the word. The "v" is the thing that messes it up. That infernal mark changes the simple trilled "r" into some amazing sound that seems to be made by trilling the "r" while at the same time producing a hiss through the front of the mouth. The two sounds are almost impossible to produce at the same time. Or take the word for "Ice Cream", which is a daunting combination of impossible sounds starting with a soft buzz followed by a shivering noise ending convulsively in a sneeze.

Next day we intended to get an early start back, but by the time the Captain had phoned everyone he wanted to say goodbye to, it was time for lunch, at which we honored the cigarette-smoking *maitre d'* at the Alcron with our final presence. Again we had four courses and left hungry.

We unlocked and removed the three gasoline cans for the trip back, packed the jeep, replaced the distributor cap, unlocked the padlock on the chain around the steering wheel and the jeep frame, filled the tank (to the envious observations of the passers-by) and were ready to set out. Then the Russian transportation system began to operate again.

This time it was a Czechoslovakian "partisan" who was hitchhiking his way across the country on "official business". The Captain engaged in spirited Czech conversation while I watched the scenery. At one point the partisan offered a salami in exchange for a package of cigarettes, a deal which we made. Later on he offered another salami and a loaf of bread for another pack, and we accepted. But he didn't have any salami or bread. He told us to stop at a bakery in a little town. He walked in, announced in a loud and threatening voice, "I am a partisan and I want one loaf of bread and two salamis and no, I don't have any food coupons, so what?", and exited without surrendering any food coupons or, indeed, any cash.

We got over the demarcation line into American territory in time for supper. We invited the partisan to join us at dinner with a GI unit to which we invited ourselves. Everybody had already eaten, so we sat down at an empty table. The partisan immediately took over. He asked rather pointedly of a Czech KP if there was any beer, and the KP hurriedly procured some, although I don't know whether anyone else had had any. He brought it in a large pitcher, which the partisan took in both of his hands and quaffed rather deeply. The Captain and I looked on amused but thirsty. But we didn't make any play at the beer. The partisan was really quite a character but seemed to be a good guy at heart. He took a great liking to us and would have deserted the Czech army in a minute and come into Germany with us if we had let him.

We drove on after supper, turning north from Pilsen instead of returning the way we had come. The Captain wanted to visit Marienbad, or Marianske Lazne, as the Czechs have renamed it, to see if the place had changed since he was last there, and more particularly to check up on the age of his girl friend in the States who was born and raised in Marienbad. He was very successful, finding out that she was 36 instead of 32 as she had always led him to believe, and that she had changed her name from Sophia to Sonja when she was eighteen. He was delighted and immediately wrote her a letter on his return to Aalen, addressing it to "Dear Sophie."

Marienbad was in American territory, and so we had some concern for our ability to find a room, it being a famous resort. But there were hundreds of hotels there. The place had nothing to offer except the springs and the baths. We found a hotel that was being vacated for Army occupancy on Monday and was therefore empty for the Saturday night we were to be there.

The Captain met some Czech people from Pilsen after we had been in Marienbad for about five minutes, and they invited us out to a place where there were to be dancing and refreshments. It was called the Kaverna Bellvue, not a bad place, with a pretty good orchestra and a liquid that looked like beer even though it had very little taste. And they had some ice cream which was not bad at all. There is where the Czech word for ice cream came up, incidentally, and I spent most of the evening muttering in my beard trying to figure out how to pronounce it.

There were two girls in the group, one of which had attached herself to a Lieutenant in the IPW of 16th Armored Division who

154

happened to be there. Another sweet young thing hung on the Captain for dear life all evening and tried to find out how she could get to America. All the girls in Czechoslovakia wanted to go to America. When the Captain told her the only way she could get there was to marry an American soldier, she hung onto him all the more, but she didn't make too much of an impression on him. Everyone gave us an address when the Bellevue closed for the night and made us promise to visit them the next time we were in Pilsen, which of course we agreed to do.

Next morning we awoke at the decent hour of nine thirty and fooled around until lunch time, when we ate with an Army unit. Then we bid goodbye to the Sudeten German who owned the hotel where we were the only guests that Saturday night, and started off for Aalen and what we call home over here. We returned without incident and with the jeep in one piece and in fairly good condition. We considered the trip on the whole a success, although the Captain had only bad news about his family.

Ludwigsburg, Bayern
1 August 1945
G e r m a n y

   We are comfortably situated in a large house on a big piece of ground planted with apple and plum trees and boasting chickens, rabbits and geese in the back acreage. We shall not do without fresh eggs in Ludwigsburg!

   The house is well-appointed, free of any war damage at all, and possessing all the necessary appliances for the good life: a refrigerator for our ample store of *Sekt* and what there is of our beer rations, adequate bathrooms if not one for every bedroom, a spacious attic where I can practice my knife-throwing although I never achieve a great deal of proficiency, two maids (one named Herte, who eyes me predatorily as though I resemble a ticket to the States), and a good German library where I can read at my leisure when I tire of the movies at night.

   Our quarters are the former abode of Their Excellencies, the Baron and Baroness Schenck zu Schweinsberg – a minor product of the pretending nobility of Germany. (The *Schweinsberg* portion of the title means "Pig Mountain" – Baron Schenck of Pig Mountain; not the most prepossessing title even in Germany.) Hitler has tolerated the nobility, even though none of his crowd is of that elite. But he has required of them, if not support, then acquiescence to the *Führer*.

   When we received orders to move to Internment Camp 73 at Kornwestheim, a suburb of Stuttgart, the Captain dispatched me and Lt. Walber to Ludwigsburg, a noble city with a magnificent palace dating from the reign of Ludwig, King of Bayern, to arrange suitable quarters for the team. Ludwigsburg is a short commute from Kornwestheim.

   When we got there we went first to the housing assignment office, where we were told that the only accommodations available were in the barracks for the EM and in the Officers' Quarters for the officers. We commented that we usually had a house for the team, but we were rebuffed by the officer rather curtly with the statement that all of the houses subject to pre-emption by our forces (which meant those houses owned or occupied by members of the NSDAP, SS, etc.) had been taken over already and were occupied. We mentioned that we had seen one lovely house on our entry into the city which seemed to still be occupied by civilians, and asked what the situation might be there.

When we described the house, he said, "Oh, that's the home of the Baron and Baroness Schenck zu Schweinsberg. They are fine people and have no affiliation that would enable us to take the house over." The way he mangled the German names, we knew he couldn't be very capable of knowing who would or would not have a guilty affiliation, but we were unable to shake his determined defense of the Baron.

Ultimately we gave up in the face of Army bureaucracy and drove back to Aalen. When we reported to the Captain, he was most upset. He excused me so he could take the Lieutenant over the coals, but I could still hear him through the door.

"Now, you say that this desirable house is owned and occupied by a *Baron*?" I could imagine him pointing his finger accusatorily at the Lieutenant. "If that is the case, I can assure you he was at least a significant member of the NSDAP. He wouldn't have been allowed to continue to live there otherwise. Didn't you tell the housing officer that?"

"Yes, we did," the Lieutenant said.

"What did he say to that?"

"He said they had investigated and found that he was not a member."

"Bullshit!" he shouted, the only time I ever heard him use such a barnyard vulgarity. "He's bound to be! I guess I'll just have to go interview the Baron myself. We are not going to live in any barracks, either you and I or the Enlisted Men. I'll go over there myself tomorrow."

It was about a three hour winding-road drive from Aalen to Ludwigsburg, and of course another three hours back. But he went, taking Levine with him. Levine was perhaps the most

157

Jewish member of our team, and the most resentful of the treatment the Jews had received at the Nazis' hands.

When they returned, they were all smiles. "We will pack and report to Ludwigsburg and Kornwestheim tomorrow," the Captain said.

"Where did you arrange for us to stay?" we asked him.

"Where else? At the residence of the Baron and Baroness Schenck zu Schweinsberg, of course. The house has not been pre-empted because he was not thought to have been a Nazi. But of course, when I interviewed him he was forced to admit that in fact he had been, and an officer, an *honorary* officer, at that. They will move to their gatehouse tomorrow, taking only their clothes and items necessary for the quietest of lifestyles. I must admit that the Baroness was not happy at all about the outcome, but that is of little concern to us. If she continues to complain, we may take the gatehouse too. But I think we shall be quite comfortable in the main house."

I didn't ask him what the housing officer had said about all this. I took it that he was quite impressed with the Captain's interviewing skill.

There are a total of 19 MIS men working at the Kornwestheim camp. We agreed to share their mess if not their accommodations. So we don't have to worry about getting rations and hiring cooks, and the food is reasonable if not up to Frau Plöschke's.

Life in Ludwigsburg is pleasant, if we could only dispel the great uncertainty that hangs over us all: when will we be sent home?

The infamous "point system" determines priority in that regard. The Captain has pursued with his usual dogged persistence the awarding of a battle star to our team for participation in the Battle of the Bulge. But remember, we moved into the Bulge area the day after the battle officially ended, so we had been refused that battle star. Now, with battle stars worth five points each toward home, we all wanted desperately to add one to the one we received for the Ruhr campaign, which is officially known as the Campaign for Central Europe. But it had all been to no avail until recently, when the Captain came back from MIS headquarters one day and announced triumphantly that we had all been awarded a battle star for the Rhineland Campaign, which presumably meant the time from the crossing of the Rhine. So now we all have 10 points for battle stars. Length of active duty service is another point determinant; marriage and a child two more. No one else on the team is married except Bob Beck, and he doesn't have a child.. I am high point man on the team.

Desire to go home doesn't add a thing, unfortunately. My revised total comes to slightly over 60 points. Soldiers having at least 60 points are at present eligible for shipping home. But there are a lot of those, and it may be a long time before the effective level reaches my total. I wait with little patience; I have never seen my eight-month old namesake nor, for nine months, my wife and the rest of my family.

Internment Camp 73 (*Stalag* or *Stammlager 73*) at Kornwestheim is a pretty good-sized camp which was formerly a German army installation. It consists mostly of a group of barracks housing the internees, plus administration buildings and some open training areas. The whole complex is surrounded by double fences of barbed wire, with guard stations at intervals. Lights cover the whole area within the fences with a brilliant glare. It is, in truth, a prison, and escapes are sometimes attempted. They seldom succeed. The camp is managed by MP units with sharpshooters stationed at the guard locations 24 hours a day. They are under orders to shoot anyone attempting an escape, and they do so with zest, having no love for the internees and no tolerance for the boredom of the job. The internees have come to fear the quick trigger fingers of the sharpshooters and only the most desperate are up to the challenge of escape. We IPWs have little to do with that aspect of the camp.

Our job is to review the files on the internees and to conduct additional interviews as thought necessary. If we determine that someone is of higher priority than our camp, we reluctantly ship

159

him off to another camp. Reluctantly, because we have heard of the treatment they are likely to receive at the higher camps: better food, better accommodations, more amenities that the commoners at our camp. They may ultimately go on to trial at Nürnberg or elsewhere, but in the meantime they live better than our lower-level folk.

The internees distinguish noticeably between the MP guards and the MIS interrogators. We treat them less harshly, giving them cigarettes on occasion (when it aids the interrogation), and providing them sometimes with insignificant but appreciated little things like chocolate K rations. When we enter the barracks the first one to see us (whether we are commissioned or not) shouts "*Achtung!*", and those highly disciplined troops snap to an attention not often seen in American barracks on the entry of an officer. Germans are very realistic in some circumstances; when their control is changed, as when they are no longer under German army control but now under American army control, they accept the change of authority almost with enthusiasm, because they feel better with *someone* in control...or at least, some of them do.

Sometimes, in the privacy of an interview, an internee will ask us to send a letter to his family to let them know where he is. Of course we are not supposed to do it, but in some instances the information is transmitted. Then, unfortunately, the family may show up at Kornwestheim and we must deny them visiting rights. But at least they know he is alive – for the time being, anyway. If they weren't all Nazis and SS troops and the like, we would feel sorry for the internees.

One somewhat sick but amusing detail: When the internees are brought into the camp, the first item of business is to debug them, that is, to get rid of the lice and fleas and other sundry insects which they often bring with them. To do this, we have them undress, give them a bar of soap, and order them as a group into the gang-showers which bear the name *Duschezimmer* (shower room) above the door. That happens to be the same title as found above the door of the gas chamber at Dachau and other concentration camps. It strikes terror into the hearts of those in the group who know about the technique of luring new prisoners into the gas chamber in the guise of taking a shower, and then gassing them all to death in an instant. Terror in the face of the *Duschezimmer* betrays internees frequently.

We work civilized hours at the camp, from 8:30 to 5:30 Monday through Saturday, with time enough off to return to Ludwigsburg to our common mess for lunch. After work hours we are free to do whatever we want – reading, going to the movies, going to sleep, maybe even going into Stuttgart to plays and operas or symphony concerts in the badly damaged but still serviceable *Stuttgart Staatsoper*. Tickets are free to American soldiers.

Ludwigsburg, Bayern
September 25, 1945
G e r m a n y

George Collier burst into my office at Camp 73 Friday afternoon, 22 September 1945. George was one of my best friends at the University of Wisconsin, the one who used to beat me badly at chess as we passed the portable board back and forth in German classes. He's from Minneapolis and Marion and I spent an interesting week-end with him there once while at Madison. He came with Murph to rescue Marion and me when we were fighting a losing fight skating against the wind on Lake Mendota in Madison.

George went through Ritchie, too. He is now with SAIC outside of Heidelberg.   SAIC stands for Seventh Army Interrogation Center, and is the place that some of our forwarded internees wind up to be interrogated in greater depth. I had no idea he was anywhere around until he suddenly appeared at the camp. He could only stay for the afternoon, but we made plans for me to come up to his place Saturday afternoon, when I could get the afternoon off. I told him I could get one of our team's jeeps and we could take a little trip around and we could see something of the country. He thought it sounded like a great idea.

Saturday I made it to Heidelberg by dinner time. George and I and a friend of George's from SAIC bummed some extra K rations and some extra gasoline and headed south along the autobahn in the direction of Karlsruhe. George's friend knew some people in Staufen, south of Freiburg, and we intended to spend the night with them.

Shortly after leaving Karlsruhe we passed into the French occupation zone. Of course, we had no orders or other valid papers. All we had was my "permanent trip ticket" which identified me as an authorized driver of the jeep at any time. Everyone on the team had one of these so people wouldn't think we had stolen the jeep. At the zone crossing point, there was one lone French soldier. We gave him a couple of cigarettes and he waved us through without even looking at my permanent trip ticket.

We got into Freiburg at about 10:30 pm. The days were still long, although it was close to the end of September, and we proceeded on about 20 kilometers to Staufen. We found the home of Collier's friend's friends just as they were preparing to go to bed. We roused them up and asked them if we could stay with them. They had no room, but the wife was a French interpreter (being a Belgian) and she knew a Captain who lived at the *Gasthaus zum Loewe*. He was very gracious and arranged to put at our disposal the only two rooms he had left.

We discovered that Staufen is the town in which the historical Faust lived, and that the *Gasthaus* where we stayed was said to have been his lodging. To cap everything off, we learned that the room in which I slept was the room in which Mephistopheles called for Faust and from which he descended to the lower regions. Having read the first part of Goethe's *Faust* in German class at Wisconsin, we knew the story. I worried all night that the horned and forktailed demon would call for me, but I was tired enough that I slept through all my worry in a wonderfully soft bed and mattress.

Next morning we arose at six o'clock and prepared for a long day. Fortunately, we didn't know how long it would really be.

The first order of business was to replenish our gasoline supply. Gasoline is supposedly not to be found in the French zone, but we were confident we could crack that nut. We inquired for the location of the nearest gasoline dump, relying solely on my less-than-perfect French. We were told there was a regimental dump in Staufen, and we sent off to investigate, with few hopes and much trepidation. We found it, with gasoline cans ("jerry cans") stacked up six or eight high in big groups. We looked for someone who could give us just a few of the plentiful cans. There was no one in evidence anywhere. The gate was open and unguarded.

Jim Hargrove

We swallowed a few times and then decided that we had a better call on the gas than black marketers. We drove up to one of the stacks of jerry cans and George hopped out and loaded three cans into the jeep. Just then a very tall, very husky, very black Senegalese French soldier appeared from nowhere and walked toward us with a rather startled expression. I was a little flustered but rose to the occasion quickly by practically throwing a pack of cigarettes at him. He started to say something but I beat him to the punch by saying in my poor French, "Take two, they're small". He looked puzzled but took the second pack and smiled broadly with beautiful white teeth.

"Merci," he acknowledged the cigarettes, and stepped aside, motioning to us to continue. We were almost to the gate when he began shouting, waving wildly and pointing to the office.

A very upset and aroused little Frenchman was emerging from the door, clad only in his underwear and swearing volubly in French, enriching my vocabulary quite a lot. When he saw that we were American soldiers, he quieted down a little. I didn't know if he was an officer or an enlisted man, since he didn't have any insignia on his undershorts. As excited as he was, I pegged him as at least a Colonel.

He was impressed by the six stripes on my arm. "Oh, excuse me," he said, "I thought you were French soldiers stealing gasoline."

I laughed at the idea. "But of a certainty, no. We are American soldiers taking gasoline." This satisfied him momentarily, but then he seemed to wonder out loud if it really made any difference what our nationality was. I hurried to explain that we were on a serious mission and had no more gas to proceed, and then, as courteously as I knew how to do, I asked if we might have just a little bit of *l'essence*.

He thought a little, shrugged his shoulders as only half-clad Gauls can do, and said "But you've already taken it, haven't you?" I agreed that such seemed to be the case. He thought a little more, then apparently decided that there were no regulations governing giving gas back to the Americans from

164

whom it had come originally. With a further Gallic shrug he commented, "What the hell, it's their gas anyway," smiled beatifically and sent us and the gasoline on our way.

I don't know how we would have gotten back to Ludwigsburg without the new gas. I'm sure no American dump would have given it to us.

We returned to Freiburg, headed east through the *Schwarzwald* (the Black Forest) toward Donaueschings, the source of the Donau (Danube) River. A little way out of Donauesching we pulled into a farmhouse, informed the people (in comfortable German, thank goodness) that we were hungry, and sat down to a country breakfast of two fried eggs apiece, a loaf of black bread, and about a pound of fresh butter. [*I was woefully but blissfully ignorant in those days of the horrors of fat and cholesterol*].

Well fortified, we then proceeded south-southeast toward the *Bodensee* (Lake Constance). We drove along the shore from Ludwigshafen to Friedrichshafen to Lindau. All the way we could see the Swiss Alps across the *Bodensee*. At Lindau we decided it was time to impose on the French again, as it was the lunch hour. We made appropriate inquiries and discovered that the *Bayerischer Hof* was the proper transient mess at which to partake of one's Sunday dinner. All one had to do was to show one's orders. We began to concoct some improbable reason why we had no orders, but by the time we arrived at the *Bayerischer Hof* we were still without any believable explanation. We needn't have worried; we simply walked into the dining room, sat down and ate a delicious dinner of steak, mashed potatoes, black bread, ice cream and two bottles of red wine. Other than being very friendly and hospitable, the people at the *Bayerischer Hof* couldn't have paid less attention to us. No one asked us for orders. Ah, the French know how to live off the land!

From Lindau we drove south through Bregenz, and along the Swiss and Lichtenstein borders to Feldkirch, where we turned once more east. There was no problem crossing into Austria, but the weather turned bad there, and from then on it was raining off and on all the time. We crossed the Alps at the Arlberg Pass. At the foot we stopped at the village of Stuben, a winter resort of note in earlier times. We dropped into the *Gasthof zur Post* in Stuben and had a cup of hot tea, since it was wet and cold outside. After visiting with the local Austrians for a while, we resumed our touristic Odyssey.

The scenery was obscured somewhat by the rain, of course, but it was nevertheless beautiful and different for a flatlander from East Texas. At Landeck we were only a couple of hours from Italy, and we debated turning right for Italy instead of keeping on our easterly course. But we would never make it back for work the next morning, we knew, so we kept our course, from Landeck to Imst, where we turned North off the Innsbruck highway to Germany and Garmisch-Partenkirchen.

Here we entered the American Zone again, coming down off Hoch Pass just as the sun was going down. We had one very nice view of the *Zugspitze* (the highest peak in Germany) before the sun set.

From Garmisch the trip was simply one of driving as fast as we could reasonably do in the wet, cold rain, and dealing with road emergencies, like the tire that went flat outside of München. We solved that when we found a motor pool repair unit where we talked a guy into exchanging our flat tire for a good one. He was willing, because it was getting late and he didn't want to have to fix it that night.

It became a race to get back for duty. We drove the autobahn through München, Augsburg, Ulm, and Stuttgart to Heidelberg, where I dropped off Collier and his friend and turned around back to Stuttgart and Ludwigsburg. I was beginning to get tired, since I had driven the open jeep almost all of the way. At 5:45 that morning I fell into bed exhausted, and left a note for the Captain that he would have to do without me that morning. He was very understanding and told the team members and our domestic staff to leave me alone. I woke up a little while ago, in mid-afternoon.

It was a pleasant little week-end jaunt. But I think I'll wait awhile before I try one like it again.

Ludwigsburg, Bayern
November 12, 1945
G e r m a n y

Life in Ludwigsburg continued in a workmanlike, regular hours, boring sort of way. Creature comforts and time off were eminently satisfactory, but beneath the calm was always the nagging wonder about getting on with our post-bellum lives.

Every now and then something occurred to break the routine.

Shortly after November 1, for instance, I went on a week's furlough trip to Switzerland. The trip was being offered widely in the American Zone. One of its primary attractions was the opportunity to call home to the States from Switzerland. Probably most of the soldiers taking the furlough went because of that. I was no exception, although I had heard that the possibility of making a connection was less than 50%, and if it was achieved the connection could be so bad that no one could understand what was said. We were in the early days of trans-Atlantic telephone communication.

But there was always the chance that things would work. Maybe I could talk to my almost year-old son.

I was dropped off at Mannheim to catch the 4:45 pm train to Mulhouse, France, where the Army had a Leave Center set up. The train trip was slow. We had supper in Karlsruhe and then proceeded to Strasbourg, now French again, where there is a sub-center for those taking the leave. After overnighting there we proceeded on to Mulhouse.

The Center was very well set up, and I concluded that the Army was really doing a decent job of arranging the furloughs. A nice Red Cross Club was available, with an upstairs writing and lounge room, a downstairs beer hall, a coffee-and-doughnuts bar, an APO, a pressing shop, a barber shop with shoe shine boys (they were PWs) and even manicurists. It was a vast improvement over the Red Cross operations I had experienced in the war.

We had to be "processed", which meant primarily converting currency to Swiss Francs and paying the stiff sum of $35 as the all-inclusive cost of the trip. In addition to the trip cost, we were allowed to bring into Switzerland the munificent sum of 200 Swiss Francs, or about $46.20 US. That number was set by the Swiss to prevent inflation from the great influx of "rich" American soldiers. All other currency we had to leave in lock boxes in Mulhouse to be picked up on our return. I didn't expect to be paying for much, anyway, except maybe a Christmas present for Marion if I could find what I wanted. The telephone calls, if any, would all be placed collect or prepaid from the States.

The phone call situation looked more promising as we prepared to leave. To avoid problems with collect calls, I decided to cable Marion to place an appointment call for my last day in Switzerland (seven days from my entry), telling her where to call me. I also asked her in the cable to tell Mother and Dad to call me in Basel at the hotel I would give her later in another cable. In addition, I would place a collect call to her as soon as I got into Switzerland, hoping to get it through before I left. Out of three chances, maybe one would work.

In one of the coincidences of war, I ran into Murphy the first day in the Mulhouse Center. Neither of us knew the other would be there. He had just returned and was headed back to Berlin a few minutes after we saw one another. Murph told me he was going to transfer from the Army to civilian status and stay in Berlin another six months at a fat salary of $3000 per year. I told him to find a lot more people who wanted to stay, then maybe I could get home quicker.

The itinerary for the leave indicated two days in Lucerne, three in Lausanne, and one each in Geneva and Basel. What in the world would I do for three days by myself in Lausanne? Shop for a watch that cost less than $45, I guessed.

So off on the trip I went. I looked at beautiful scenery, although it was a little late for the summer season and a little early for the winter season. I ate civilian meals at the hotels because I didn't have money enough to go to outside restaurants, I went to a picture show or two, and I searched diligently for a watch for Marion for Christmas. Finally I found one, had it wrapped for Christmas, and hid it securely in my small carry-on bag when I got back to the hotel. In Geneva I went with my friend from Ludwigsburg to a night club (the *Club d'Hiver*) which had an orchestra, and an area where people could dance. I didn't want to dance with my friend from Ludwigsburg, so the dance floor went unused as far as we were concerned. There was also a fair floor show, and a bar which had good and cheap (very important!) beer.

We got into Basel at about 1 pm the last day. I immediately notified the hotel (it was the Continental, not the *Schweitzerhof* as I had cabled Marion) that I was expecting two telephone calls from the States. Just as I got through with lunch the clerk came into the restaurant and told me that my call was coming through. I went out and took it in a little booth (of course I didn't have a phone in my room). Until I heard Dad's voice I didn't know which call had come through. But even though I couldn't ask to speak to my son, I did get quite a kick out of talking to everyone. I could have gone about ten minutes more, but that might have bankrupted Dad.

I tried to get some information on my call from Marion, but none had come through. I wondered about my collect call, but that was supposed to be so uncertain I didn't give it much chance. At about 11 pm I went to bed and told the porter to call me if my call came through. At about 2 a.m. he called me that it was coming, and I ran downstairs to take it. But the connection was impossible. We shouted at one another; I'm sure the rest of the people in the hotel heard me, but Marion couldn't. The static was overpowering.

I wasn't happy about the failure of the call, but there wasn't anything I could do about it. I went back upstairs and to bed. The next morning we left Switzerland and returned to Mulhouse, then to Ludwigsburg and the routine again of high living, leisure time, and boredom.

170

Stuttgart, Bayern
26 November 1945
G e r m a n y

I am no longer in the Military Intelligence Service. In a revolutionary turn of lifestyle, I am now an infantry unit GI, a member of Company F, 397th Infantry Regiment, 100th Infantry Division. Amid my fellow GIs, my six-striped shirt looks quite out of place – or it would if the whole unit didn't consist of out-of-place GIs.

The 100th Infantry has been designated a demobilization unit, designed to take eligible men from their service units, process them and cuddle them in its bureaucratic arms, and take them home. I am beginning my journey to Shreveport. And like every other man in the division, I don't care what the unit looks like or does, as long as it moves us westward with dispatch.

Bob Beck and I were notified on November 22 that we would be transferred to a unit "for transportation to the United States and discharge from the service." Beautiful words, pure poetry. We left Ludwigsburg the next day for Seventh Army Headquarters at Heidelberg, where we picked up our orders and records and had our flu shots. There were about 40 MIS men in our shipment, but only four, including Beck and me, in Company F. Then we came back to Stuttgart, where Company F is located, and checked into a house with a bunch of others being transferred as we were. We chowed with Company F, then caught a ride to Ludwigsburg, only 20 miles away, and returned to the IPW group in time for soup and a dessert with them. Afterward, the Captain drove us back to Company F and deposited us at our temporary home, to awe-struck observations from real GIs who had never been chauffeured by a Captain.

Next day we were included in a guard roster and walked guard until someone decided it didn't look good to have a Master Sergeant walking guard, after which I was relieved. Bob Beck, of course, was not excused, having only two stripes on his sleeves. After lunch he and I took off again for Ludwigsburg, using the ever-present and friendly free transportation available always in the form of jeeps going there and back. After dinner I came back to Stuttgart with the Captain and we went to an opera – *"Orfeus und Eurydike"* – which was different and well-done. We returned to Ludwigsburg and I supervised the preparation of some chili and scrambled eggs, using the chili I had received in my Christmas packages from home. The combination was new to him, but very old to my Southwestern heritage. He seemed to like it. Beck and I then returned to Stuttgart by hitchhiking, the Captain having had enough trips to Stuttgart for the day.

And so went life in the Infantry. We spent most of our time in Ludwigsburg gloating over the others still there, and we beat a path to the Stuttgart *Staatstheater*, seeing just about everything they produced. I improved my classical music background considerably. Beck and I, accompanied sometimes by the Captain or others from Ludwigsburg, witnessed, in addition to *Orfeus und Eurydike, Die Fledermaus,* Schiller's *Don Carlos* (all four hours of it), and *Die Hochzeit des Figaro*, together with *Ingeborg* and a number of other plays, and several symphony concerts. I couldn't get over the number of operas in their repertory. American soldiers had the best seats in the house reserved for them, in the loges and boxes, and it was all free. The company was subsidized by the city of Stuttgart, and had been stable for many years, enabling them to produce such a large number of events.

The processing for return home included a check of our required shots. My flu shots that I had taken when I checked out of Seventh Army had not gotten on my record, and they insisted I had to take them again if I wanted to leave with them. Despite my protestations, they would not relent, and I sure didn't want to get left in Stuttgart. So I took the flu shots again. I had only a modest reaction to the double shot and recovered from my inoculation promptly. Double protected, I withstood the abnormally cold weather well. We had taken on "DS"("Detached Service") an electric heater which I am sure the Baron and Baroness Schenck zu Schweinsberg wanted us to have, and that, running constantly day and night to augment the one wood stove built into our house, kept us from freezing, if not making us completely comfortable.

Jim Hargrove

Marseilles, France
16 December 1945

In retrospect, the trip was not that bad.

But while we were on it, it was. How long ago had I first heard of the "40 & 8"s? The legendary troop transports of the French railway system, designed to carry in boxcars a maximum of 40 men or 8 horses? I think Dad first mentioned them, although I'm not sure he ever really rode in one.

I did. It was the deluxe version, though – we only had 20 men per car, and, fortunately, no horses at all. In one corner was a wood potbellied stove, which looked inadequate to the challenges of the winter but proved to be effective so long as all 20 of us crowded into its corner. On the floor for our lounging and sleeping comfort and our convenience in not having to police the floor every day, was a generous heap of straw. I was a little concerned about burning the place up, given the straw and the white-hot stove, but we took care not to let the straw get very close to the fire, and it never caught. Besides, at the speed we traveled, it would have always been possible to open the sliding door and jump off the train without much fear of injury. How do you stretch a train ride over about 500 miles into four days and four nights? By creeping, that's how. And creep we did. The creeping pace had another advantage: the snow didn't blow in around the door when we went that slow.

I looked in vain for evidence of plumbing facilities. Four days and nights without plumbing? I asked one of the cadre how we were going to get by without it. "Oh, you can brush your teeth and shave out of your helmets," he offered.

I pointed out that we had all checked-in our helmets long ago and taken to wearing the soft overseas caps.

"Well, then spit out the door when you brush your teeth and don't shave until we get there," he said, turning to take care of another domestic crisis. I pointed out that there were other uses for the plumbing than brushing one's teeth. "Out the door," he

174

replied tersely, "and we'll stop often enough for you to take care of any other requirements."

OK, I could work with that. One thing I sure didn't need to do was shave. When we finally got to Marseilles, I looked like a youthful Santa Claus. I remembered how my great-grandfather looked in his Civil War era full beard. Maybe if I didn't shave on the boat either I could look like he did by the time we reached New York. Then I remembered how as a little boy I hated to have to kiss him, and I gave up the idea.

My first moments in our new home at the Port of Embarkation were devoted to shaving and showering to remove the fuzzy beard and an inexhaustible amount of coal soot and dirt of various sorts which had found every nook and cranny of my body to hide in.

One of the first things I had to do was check in at the med station for a flu shot. I got upset this time. "I've had two flu shots in the last few weeks," I protested. No avail. Not on my record. They couldn't take my word for it. Roll up your sleeve. Bang, it's over with. I get a little more of the inoculation flu, but again I'm cured quickly. I am now absolutely full of the antibodies, and, except for the fact that it's the Army medical system doing it, I'd be confident I wouldn't get the flu for a while.

In the Port of Marseilles we are quartered in winterized tents – 16 of us to a tent. This leaves something to be desired in the area of privacy, but no one complains much about the lack of appropriate ambiance. Bob Beck rode in the same 40 & 8 with me, and now is in the same tent. We have become good friends and find some comfort in being able to bitch to one another about how much better it was in MIS.

The Red Cross is active with clubs and lounges, although they're not up to the standards of the Mulhouse Leave Center. No matter; we are but transitory pilgrims making our way slowly and not very steadily homeward. Discomfort and frustration roll as easily off our backs as the proverbial water does off a duck's back. We are impervious.

Port of Embarkation
22 December 1945
Marseilles, France

Perhaps not as impervious as I thought.

We were told yesterday that we were scheduled to depart Marseilles 25 December, (Christmas Day!) on the former cruise liner *Vulcania*, renamed from *La Contessa di Savoia*. Its capacity is 3773 troops, a few more than its capacity as a cruise liner, to be sure. It is capable of reaching New York from Marseilles in 7½ days, considerably faster than the converted Victory ships that are also in the business of transporting troops across the Atlantic. The Victory ships, like their earlier counterparts the Liberty ships, were designed for freight, not people, and the troop-carrying facilities with which they have been fitted are not designed with creature comfort in mind.

We were put on departure alert yesterday for a scheduled departure today. But that was spiked at noon by the announcement that we would ship the 25th instead. Today at noon it was announced that there has been a further 3-day delay; we will now ship out December 28. Our vaunted patience was punctured cruelly. Christmas on a luxury cruise liner would certainly have been preferable to one here in a tent shared with 15 other men. But, after all, we are only a few days from home.

Be patient.
Be patient.
Be patient...

Port of Embarkation
29 December 1945
Marseilles, France

We were alerted day before yesterday for an embarkation on the 28th. A few hours before we were to embark, a company formation was called and we were there informed that we would not board the *Vulcania* that day as previously stated. Our earliest possible shipping date had been changed to January 8 because *the Vulcania had been diverted to Le Havre to take elements of the 82nd Airborne Division to New York in time to participate in a parade for "GI Joe Day", a celebration honoring the noble and brave citizen soldiers who had won the war!*

Now, the 82nd Airborne was a veteran unit, composed of true soldiers who had suffered a great deal in combat. But it had been selected, as the 100th Infantry had also, as a vehicle to transport home soldiers eligible for discharge. The 82nd Airborne was no longer the same unit that fought so fiercely in the war. Instead it consisted of dischargees who had points in the 50s range – compared to the 100th Infantry, whose present members had point counts in the 60s range.

If they wanted someone to march in the parade, we would have volunteered – provided it didn't delay our discharge from the Army.

I and my fellow infantrymen were shocked, stunned, incredulous, bitter, vindictive and otherwise generally unhappy Oh, we knew for a certainty that we could do nothing about it. But we tried anyway.

That afternoon about 3000 men of the 397th Regiment marched over to the IG's office (that's the Inspector General, whose job it is to investigate any questionable incident) and laid our complaints before him. Of course we got nothing but conciliatory pap, protests of inability to do anything about it, and a couple of lies (for example, the statement of a Transportation Corps Lieutenant that the *Vulcania* had sprung five main plates and was in port for repairs, a statement we all knew to be patently false).

But we had made our point, and we accepted the fact of our incapacity to alter fate.

I must lay a predicate for what we did next.

There was a lot of non-exchangeable "occupation currency" running around the camp. This came from a number of sources, some not really illegal, like gambling winnings, and others clearly illegal, like the black market. We all had notations in our pay records as to how much "occupation currency" we had been issued officially. This amount was exchangeable to dollars. Anything above that was not eligible for exchange and was therefore worthless.

One of the favorite pastimes at the POE was gambling. The gambling was conducted in the only currency most people had, that is, occupation currency. Since that money could not be taken home and used, it was worth very little or, in most cases, nothing. It could be used for some purposes, though. Flowers and candy and birthday or Christmas presents, things like that could be paid for at the POE and sent to people in the States by wire, using the facility established by Western Union. Some girl friends got enormous bouquets of flowers and boxes of chocolates as a result; mothers who might not have heard from their sons in a long time were suddenly inundated with costly corsages or table flowers.

And it could be used to send cables.

Last night a very long cablegram was composed and sent to 10 addressees in the States, including President Truman, Senator Mead, Walter Winchell, the editors of three New York City newspapers, the Speaker of the House, and one or two others. It told our woeful story. It was paid for by an unofficial levy against all the poker winnings in the 397th Regiment. Others offered to contribute, but they were refused because they involved "real money" instead of "poker money". It was the gamblers' *beau geste* for their non-gambling buddies in the Regiment.

Of course, it was full of sound and fury, but signified nothing. We would ship out no sooner than ten days hence.

Aboard the *SS Cody Victory*
Off Hoboken, New Jersey, USA
13 January 1946

Maybe I was wrong about the lack of significance in our voluble protests. We were told that 8 January was the earliest we could expect to ship out after the *Vulcania* was diverted. But in fact we boarded the *SS Cody Victory* on 2 January, six days earlier than expected. True, it was a Victory ship, not a cruise liner, and it took us eleven days to cross from Marseilles to New York Harbor. It seemed forever to us.

Life began to get a little back to a civilian perspective as soon as we boarded. Everything was American – ship, food, language, outlook, etc. It wasn't fancy at all. And it was not really able to take care of 3000 guests without sacrificing a little lifestyle.

For one thing, the dining facilities were grossly inadequate. Breakfast came very early in the morning, but it was served in a cafeteria line and we could really have about as late a breakfast as we wanted if we just waited to get into the line until about 10 o'clock. That was as late as you could wait because if you didn't get in line by that time, they started serving the other meal of the day at about 12, and you didn't have a prayer of making it to the food counter before the breakfast line became a dinner line. Since there were only two meals a day, we had to eat 1½ times as much as normal per meal in order to get the equivalent of three meals. Most of us had no trouble with that.

But some did. When we boarded ship, a friend from the 397th Regiment offered me his meal card. That meant I could eat four times a day if I hurried.

"Aren't you going to use it?" I asked.

"No, I won't be needing it. I'm reporting to the infirmary and I'll be there for the whole trip."

"But we haven't even cast off yet," I protested. "Look, the lines are still attached to the dock. The boat's not moving at all. How could you be seasick?"

"Do you want the meal card or not? I'm already seasick and I know I'm going to be much worse before we get there. I have no use for it."

"OK, thanks," I gave up. "I'll see how good the cuisine is before I double up."

I looked at the half-empty package of cigarettes in my hand. I had started smoking again when we left New York over a year ago, mostly to have something to do and also, Scotch as I am, to avail myself of the bargain of cigarettes for nothing most of the time, and for 5 cents a pack other times. I knew what Marion thought of my smoking, and I had to agree with her on principle. I looked around and found a friend who I knew was a smoker.

"Here, you can have these," I offered. "I'm not going to need them any more."

"Are you quitting?" he asked.

"Yes."

"Don't you want to keep them until we get to New York? It's going to be a long trip anyway, but without cigarettes it would be forever."

"It will be forever anyway," I closed the conversation. And I quit smoking.

Most of the time Bob Beck and I played checkers. I think I won more often than I lost. He thought he won more often than he lost. Actually, we didn't keep track of who won or who lost. It was just a way to get from daylight to dark. Most of the time we played on deck, often while we were waiting in the breakfast or the dinner line.

I read, too — again on deck where I could escape the claustrophobia. I didn't read anything worthwhile, just time-passers. They did help to pass the time and give me a little respite from the constant contest with Beck.

We encountered the American coast somewhere in the Carolinas and turned north to New York. I didn't wholly understand why we couldn't dock in any of the quite adequate ports along the lower east coast, but of course there were lots of things I never understood during my army time. After a couple

181

of days we reached the New York Harbor area and lay to overnight. I heard we were going into Hoboken, and then to Camp Kilmer, where they would put together a troop train to take us Louisiania and Mississippi lads to a separation center at Camp Shelby, near Hattiesburg, Mississippi. They said we would only be in Kilmer for two days at the most. I hope I have time to make some phone calls – some with a better connection than Switzerland had.

Camp Shelby, Mississippi
January 18, 1946

For once, the Army had made an accurate estimate. We docked in Hoboken, clambered down the gangplank to the applause of a modest crowd, most of whom were there to greet their men on return from the war. I had told Marion not to come because I didn't expect to have any free time at Camp Kilmer, but others who were close came to cheer and cry. I felt a little like doing both myself.

Kilmer looked not much different than it had, except there was lots less baggage around to be put on our shoulders as we marched to the train for an overseas departure. As soon as we were given a barracks assignment I ran to a telephone bank at the Rec Center and with shaking hands dialed zero for a collect call to Houston, Hadley 1644. The phone rang only once and then I heard a voice I took to be Marion's, even though it sounded so like someone out of the kitchen of Tara that I had a hard time believing it was my wife.

"My gosh, I never heard such a Southern accent," I said. "Are you sure this is Marion Smith Hargrove?"

"It's me all right," she drawled, using up expensive telephone time in the one phrase, "but who is the gentleman from Brooklyn who is calling?"

"Surely you can recognize your own husband," I protested.

"Well, I bet your Jewish friends don't sound as Southern as you sound Jewish. They seem to have converted you completely. Are you speaking English or Yiddish?"

"Enough of the chatter," I shut the banter off, "now let's have a real conversation."

The rest of the conversation is not to be shared.

The troop train moved almost as slowly as the 40 & 8 train from Stuttgart to Marseilles. Rocking along to let us have a good look at the country on the way, once more with open windows (even if it was January), and blowing soot over everything, we chugged our way through Virginia, Tennessee,

183

Alabama, and finally Mississippi, through Hattiesburg and to the dreary but beautiful (to us) camp where we would be honorably separated from the Army of the United States. As soon as I was shown a barracks, I dashed again to the phone bank and put in another call to Marion, this time in Shreveport, where she had come with Jimmy, ready to leave him with Mother and Dad.

I told her to come right away to the hotel in Hattiesburg. I would get off as soon as I could, probably the next night, and meet her at the hotel. That arranged, and having talked to Mother and Dad, I went to the barracks, showered the soot and dirt from hair and body, and slept. My last thought before sleeping: "What if they won't give me a pass tomorrow night?"

I checked in early to the First Sergeant's office. He was on the phone, his back to me when I walked in. On his desk were several pads of blank passes. I reverted back almost three years, recalling Camp Wallace, and quietly pocketed a book of blanks. When he finished his talk, I asked him if passes were available for the night. "Of course!" he beamed. "Where do you think you are, in the Army?" I thanked him sincerely but did not move to return the pilfered passes. One could never tell.

Separation was mostly checking records, filling out forms, agreeing to continue my National Service Life Insurance, and resisting the high-pressure attempts to get me to enlist in the Reserves. I had a great future there, the recruiter assured me, and if there should ever be another conflict where the Reserves would be called up, I could expect to be given a shot at Officers' Candidate School immediately. I let my mind drift backward to my time in Europe. What could I have had as a Lieutenant that would have been as good as a Sergeant in a *gemütlich*, independent, separately quartered and rationed unit like IPW Team 138, where the greatest danger I would run would be a disabling wound to my middle pinkie so I couldn't type? I thought the exalted rank of Lieutenant would have been a big step downward.

"No thanks, Sergeant," I said. "I don't think I'm cut out for a commission."

Finally all my processing was ended. I was told that tomorrow I would be given my discharge and my back pay and I could be on my way, free and civilian.

The next day I hopped a bus to Hattiesburg. A very young soldier boarded when I did. Camp Shelby was a Reception Center as well as a Separation Center. I decided he was a new inductee. It was a shock to realize the Selective Service System was still operating. I took the book of blank passes out of my pocket.

"Here," I proffered the book to him. "Do you want these?"

He looked at the book of passes, reading it slowly, either for care or because he wasn't a very good reader. "What would I do with them?" he asked. I was quiet for a while, remembering what I had done with them. "Never mind," I answered. "I don't think you would do anything with them."

I threw them into a trash bin at the bus station.

I reached the hotel about 4:30 in the afternoon and inquired for Marion's room. The clerk looked it up and, in the trusting environment of the day and of Hattiesburg, he gave me the number without calling up to the room. Heart pounding, breathing shallowly, hands sweating lightly, I took the elevator up to her floor, located her room, and stopped outside the door for a minute of gathering myself together. Then I turned the knob (it wasn't locked) and opened the door.

She was sitting in the chair pretending to read a book. She was beautiful. She looked up when I entered and squinted to make sure it was really me. For a moment neither of us moved. Then she jumped up from her chair, ran to me and hugged me tightly. "Oh, Jim, I'm so glad you're back!" she cried.

And so was I. So was I.

Jim Hargrove

Appendices

Jim Hargrove

HEADQUARTERS, XVI CORPS ARTILLERY
IPW TEAM 138
APO 197
US ARMY

12 May 1945

SUBJECT : Sidelights on Nazi Germany.

TO: : Scoffs, G-2, Hq, XVI Corps, APO 197, U. S. Army (Thru Channels).

1. Following sidelights of events in Nazi Germany during the past year have been obtained from Wilhelm Rohrssen, Georgstrasse 18, Bueckeburg, Germany, who for four and a half years was Major Domo in several of the State Guest Houses in Berlin.

2. Attached reports deal with:

   a. Biography of Wilhelm Rohrssen

   b. The Story of 20 July 1944

   c. 10 December 1944

   d. Hitler's Physician Shot

Jim Hargrove

    e.   The Last Putsch

    f.   Where is Hitler's Body?

    g. CI Targets

GEORGE D. BUXBAUM
Capt, QMC
CIC, IPW Team 132

CONFIDENTIAL

Biography of Wilhelm Rohrssen, Schlossoberinspektor

I, Chief Castle Inspector (*Schlossoberinspektor*) Rohrssen, was born on 4 January 1888 in Altenhagen, in the vicinity of Schaumberg, Lippe. I learned the profession of *Haushofmeister* (Major Domo or Master-of-Estate) in the imperial castle in the vicinity of Berlin, at the Ducal Courts in Dessau and Altenberg. Having passed examination, I was employed in Bueckeburg as *Haushofmeister* for the reigning Elector, Adolph zu Schaumberg Lippe. After the Revolution of 1918 I was appointed *Schlossoberinspektor* and administered the seven castles of the Elector. In addition I was manager for the hotels in Bad Eilson.

In the summer of 1935, on the occasion of a visit of a traveling party of *Kraft durch Freude* members, I had a run-in with the travel guide of the party, who wanted things done his own way in the castle. As a result of this disagreement, I was called to the provincial government a few days later. There I was informed that in the next few days I could count on being taken off to a concentration camp. Through the personal intervention of the Prince Adolph and Count Henkel-Donnergnark, I escaped this fate.

In March 1936, while on a tour of the world, the last reigning Prince of my castles was killed in an airplane accident in Mexico. I was remembered in his will. The testament was carried out and I was pensioned. I continued my service, however, for special remuneration.

In 1937 I received a notice from the NSDAP to the effect that I should declare my intention of joining the Party as a member. To avoid the many inconveniences to which I as a known reactionary was always exposed, I resolved finally to join up. My resolve was decided by the announcement of the Estate

Administration that only Party members could remain in permanent employ.

Both before and after the persecution of the Jews, I maintained relations with my old acquaintances, among whom were the Jewish banker Meyer and the merchant Northeim. Inasmuch as Meyer, the banker, came to my office almost every day, and this was observed by the woman party member Crassman, I was one day called to account by the *Ortsgruppenleiter*. That led to my official renunciation of my candidacy for Party membership. My action was answered in writing by the Party, to the effect that I was not deemed worthy of acceptance into the Party as a member.

After the occupation of Belgium in 1940, a commission arrived in Bueckeburg, consisting of *Reichsminister* Speer, *Staatsminister* Meissner, *Landespräsident* Dreyer, *Gauleiter* Meyer, and others. The commission was charged by Hitler with the mission of determining whether the castle of Bueckeburg could be considered a suitable place of internment for the Belgian king. On the occasion of the visit, I was made responsible by Meissner for the household management for the king. After some time, Meissner came again to Bueckeburg. The entire plan was changed. Meissner relieved me of my responsibilities, then inquired about my history and my entire activity at the Court. Upon departure, Meissner said: "We can use such a man in Berlin."

But I had little enthusiasm for the prospect of service in Berlin, as I had in Bueckeburg my good income and also my property. It is therefore easy to understand that I had a hard time tearing myself loose from my place of work, where I had served the Royal House almost 30 years. In September 1940 I received a telegram from Meissner to report in Berlin. There I was introduced to the Foreign Minister, to Dr. Goebbels, and to some other gentlemen. My future job was described to me as extremely desirable. Again I should be *Haushofmeister*. Soon after my return from Berlin, two officials of the Reich Government came and negotiated with the estate administration

192

for my release. The estate administration fought back with every means. When no accord could be reached, the officials stated, "If you don't release Rohrssen voluntarily, we will use force, and order him to start in his new job in Berlin the 22nd of October." Just about that time I suffered several serious blows of fate in Bueckeburg, the most serious of which was the death of my wife. The parting from the vicinity was therefore made easier for me.

In Berlin I administered the real estates at Hermann Goering Strasse, Lanke, Schwänenwerder, and Castle Bellevue. I also was in charge of the receptions at these houses, supervised the personnel, and was responsible for the food and drinks. Everything was to be done in a nobleman's way. Unfortunately, I soon experienced great disappointment in my Berlin job. The behavior of the guests absolutely did not conform to what I had formerly been used to. My whole position there was so disgusting to me that I gave notice after four weeks. After I had again been threatened with an obligation to work, I had to resign myself to the fact that I could not get free for some time.

After a while I was asked to join the Party by the personal adjutant of Dr. Goebbels. I refused flatly with the reasoning that I had already been pronounced unworthy by the Party in Bueckeburg. I also know of anonymous letters, addressed to the Party directorate at Berlin, from Party members in Bueckeburg, stating that they could not understand why I, a well-known reactionary, had been given such a position. The whole affair concerning admission to the Party soon faded away, and I never heard of it again. I must mention, however, that I was constantly watched by the Gestapo, members of which were in the house. Not quite a year ago the personal data of my whole family were examined by the *Geheimdienst* in Bielefeld. I was under constant surveillance. Every unguarded statement could be fatal to me.

On 10 December 1944, Hitler was at the house in Hermann Goering Strasse for the last time. In my opinion Hitler was a gravely ill man, hardly able to control his speech and senses, owing to the attempt on his life 20 July 1944. I personally had a short conversation with him. I was astonished to see that such a wreck of a man was at the helm of a nation.

In my function as Major Domo, I remained in the house in Hermann Goering Strasse until the common death, through poisoning, of the whole Goebbels family and its entourage. I escaped sharing the same fate only by jumping through the window and fleeing. I am in all probability the only survivor.

The Story of 20 July 1944

On 20 July 1944, guests had been invited to a dinner in the State House in Hermann Goering Strasse, Berlin, where I had served since 1940 in the capacity of Major Domo. Goebbels, who was at the time residing at the house, had come home from the Propaganda Ministry about 3:00 o'clock that afternoon, as was his usual practice. The dinner was planned for 8:00 o'clock.

At about 5:30 in the afternoon, I went into the kitchen to check up on the preparations for dinner. What I saw there astonished me greatly. The entire room was seething with excitement, the various chauffeurs and servants in the house (who were almost without exception SS men) were loading submachine guns which they evidently had been given, and the cook seemed to be in a very frightened state. "What in the world is going on here?" I cried. "Don't you see?" replied the cook. "The whole house is surrounded." I looked out of the window where she pointed and saw the members of the Guard Battalion (who were charged with the garrisoning and protection of the Berlin area) standing in a ring around the house with fixed bayonets. In the house SD (*Sicherheitsdienst)* men were standing at every window with submachine guns and pistols. I went up to the third floor, where I could look out on the surrounding district. There I saw that the street was blocked off with tanks and other army vehicles; field kitchens had even been set up. The street-cars were running past the house empty; no pedestrians were allowed in the area.

Some few minutes later an SD man came up to me and said, "Get yourself a pistol and take a post at one of the windows." I refused, saying, "No, why should I? No one is going to do anything to us."

During the afternoon and early hours of the evening a great number of Party officials came to the house from Berlin, passing through the cordon with the red Party banners as passes. Shortly before 7:00 p.m. a Major Rehmer, CO of the Guard Bn, came in to the house to talk with Goebbels. Upstairs (so it was described to me by others who were actually there) Rehmer explained to Goebbels what the situation was, that Hitler was dead, and that he had the mission from General von Hase (Commander of the Berlin garrison) to occupy the government district. I do not believe Rehmer was very well informed on the situation as it actually was, and I do not believe he knew actually what he was supposed to do. When Goebbels heard Rehmer's story, he phoned by private wire to the Supreme Headquarters in the Field, which was located at the time near Marienburg, in East Prussia. He asked to talk to Hitler. After a short delay Hitler came to the phone and spoke to Goebbels. Goebbels then handed the receiver to Rehmer, who talked personally with the Führer. Hitler ordered Rehmer to take steps immediately to beat down all resistance to the Führer. Rehmer, shaken by his conversation with a man he thought dead, complied.

A few minutes later Goebbels and Rehmer came downstairs. Rehmer called in half of the men of his Guard Battalion and assembled them in the courtyard. There Goebbels delivered a very inflammatory speech ordering them to resist any and all attempts to depose the Führer and his clique. Rehmer followed up with a speech confirming what Goebbels had said. Then the men were taken outside again and the other half was brought in. The speech-making was repeated. As Goebbels and Rehmer turned to go inside, I hear Goebbels say to Rehmer, "Now we are once more masters of the situation. In a few hours they (the

Generals who had inspired the plot) will all be cold." The soldiers remained in the vicinity until the next afternoon, when they were withdrawn.

About 9:00 p.m. Himmler arrived at the house. Shortly thereafter General von Hase and his Adjutant, a Colonel, arrived at the house under guard. They were taken upstairs, where they were interrogated by Goebbels and Himmler. When the first interrogation was through, they came back downstairs and were put in a room under guard of two SS men. An SS man came to me and ordered me to go to General von Hase, whom I knew very well. Von Hase was a very fine man, a soldier of the old school; not such an upstart as Sepp Dietrich, Waffen SS Commander, whom I heard one time remark that he regretted having been unable to visit the Suez Canal when he was in France.

When I reported to General von Hase, he asked me for a bottle of wine. I brought him this, and he then asked me if I could bring him a few cigarettes. These I also brought him. His weapons and decorations had been taken away from him, and I could see he was a beaten man. His adjutant, the Colonel, was leaning on the table, his face in his hands, weeping. Later on the General asked for another bottle of wine, which I brought him. He and his adjutant stayed there until early morning, being interrogated by Himmler and Goebbels several more times during the night. About 5:00 a.m. the General, still accompanied by his Adjutant, was taken away by the SS men. On his way out, he stopped to shake hands with me, visibly shaking. He turned hurriedly after this goodbye and got into the waiting car.

Other Generals were also brought in during the night and interrogated, along with various other high-ranking army officers. Among the generals I recognized Generalmajor Kurzfleisch and Generaloberst Fromm. Fromm I also knew well – when I brought him a glass of water once during the night he was weeping like a child.

Once a major was brought in by the SS. He was complaining loudly, "What is the meaning of this? I was brought in here and all of my things were taken away from me by a simple SS man!" Whereupon an SS Lieutenant shouted at him, "Stand over there in the corner! You are now our prisoner!"

That evening, about 12:00 midnight, Hitler spoke over the radio to let the people know he was still alive. The plot was ended; the attempt had failed.

The rumors about Colonel Staufenberg and General Beck are generally known. My version of the course of events in Hitler's Headquarters comes from *Hauptsturmführer* Eckholt, of the SD. According to him, the following is the story of the actual assassination attempt:

A military conference was scheduled for 20 July in Hitler's Headquarters near Marienburg in East Prussia. A specially built concrete bunker was supposed to be the scene of the conference, but it was not ready when the day of the affair arrived, and the meeting was changed to one of the rooms of the barracks nearby. The room was fitted with a round conference table in the center of the room; on one wall was hung a large map.

Colonel Staufenberg (who was Liaison Officer between the Home Army and the Field Army) arrived as the conference was beginning. He walked up to the table, laid some papers on the table, and leaned his briefcase against one of the table legs. This done, he turned around and walked out of the room. As he left, Hitler got up from the table and walked over to the map on the wall. As he was pointing to the map and lecturing his officers, the bomb, concealed in the briefcase, exploded. Colonel Staufenberg was already outside in his car, leaving for the airfield where he had an airplane ready. The blast of the bomb blew out the windows and wrecked the room, killing several of the assembled officers and wounding others. Hitler was also wounded, although the seriousness of his wounds did not appear until later.

The would-be assassins remained for some while unknown. Finally, however, a telegraphist revealed he had seen Staufenberg leaving the area in his car at the time of the blast.

For this information the telegraphist was rewarded with RM 30,000 and his own home.

Staufenberg landed at Staaken near Berlin and proceeded to the Headquarters OKW in Sandlerstrasse in Berlin. Here he met other high ranking army officers, among whom were Kitzleben, and Beck. He reported Hitler as dead. Shortly thereafter, however, the headquarters was attacked by SS and Gestapo men. Staufenberg, seeing the situation was hopeless, shot himself. Beck also shot himself, but he did not die immediately. General Fromm gave him the *coup de grace*. In the battle which took place between the SS, together with the Gestapo, and these army officers, many were killed. Those who were not were arrested and, together with other officers implicated later, tried before the People's Court, presided over by Dr. Preis. This court condemned the officers to death by hanging. They were hanged in groups of six. Dr. Goebbels always had eye-witnesses present at the hangings, and the executions were filmed. Two of Goebbels' witnesses were Wachter and Hinkel, both high-ranking SS men.

The method of hanging was unique and ghastly, as described to me by a witness to the showing of one of the films. The six men to be executed were led out to a bank, where a rope and pulley arrangement had been erected. The hands of the condemned were tied behind them. One by one they were led under the noose. There a huge brute of a man fastened the noose around their necks and signaled to another man who pulled the noose tight around the neck. The great executioner then lifted the victims in a bear hug. The slack was taken up in the rope. The executioner then jerked down on the body with all of his brute force, breaking the victim's neck. In order to make sure the neck was broken, a third man came up and struck the victim a sharp blow on the jaw, twisting the head in such a manner as to insure the severing of the vertebrae in the back of the neck.

10 December 1944

The first and only time I saw Hitler after the 20 July 1944 attempt on his life was 10 December 1944, when he came to the house of Hermann Goering Street to a tea. He was a broken man, very sick, and apparently in a disturbed mental condition. He walked with a halting, shuffling gait, bent over, and had a very difficult time taking off his coat. I was astonished at the change in him since the last time I had seen him. My wife was equally disturbed. "And this is the leader of the German people?" she asked. "Poor Germany!"

Hitler's Physician Shot

About the middle of April 1945, I witnessed another dramatic episode in the house in Hermann Goering Street. At that time Dr. Brand, for years the personal physician of Hitler, was tried and condemned for disloyalty to the Führer.

Brand was charged with failure to carry out the orders of the Führer to evacuate his wife and family to the Redoubt at Berchtesgaden. Brand had instead moved them to the West, that they might come under the "protection" of the invading Western Allies. Furthermore, Brand was charged with confiding to a friend that he himself intended to flee from Berlin and give himself up to these same Allies. In consequence of these charges, in disobedience to the Führer, Brand was condemned to death and shot. Brand had long been the antagonist of Dr. Conti, National Health Inspector, who owed his rise to prominence to his treatment of Horst Wessel, the Nazi martyr. These two physicians, together with Dr. Morel, also a personal physician of the Führer, were the highest medical men, politically speaking, in Germany.

The Last *Putsch*

On Friday, 21 April 1945, Hitler's birthday (he was 56 years old), at about 10:30 p.m., Frau Magda Goebbels and her six children moved from their residence in Schwänenwerder to the bunker behind the house in Hermann Goering Street. The move was made on Goebbel's orders. Early the next morning, Saturday, I drove to Schwänenwerder to bring the servants for the children.

At Schwänenwerder I met Goebbels' mother-in-law, Frau Behrend, who appeared quite nervous and distraught. When she saw me, she came to me and said, "Herr Rohrssen, we are seeing each other for the last time. I believe it is all over." I protested, in order to quiet her down. "Oh, I don't think it is as bad as that!" She was not consoled; instead she continued by saying, "These last few hours I would like to be with my daughter, but the Minister (Goebbels) has forbidden it." (Goebbels did not get along too well with his mother-in-law). Still attempting to quiet her, I promised, "When I get back I will speak to your daughter about the matter, and perhaps it can be arranged." She was overjoyed at the prospect. "Oh, if you can do that I will be eternally thankful to you," she cried. She evidently did not think it could be worked out, however, because when I left the sounds of her weeping could be heard over the whole house.

This conversation with Frau Behrend together with the fact that the whole Goebbels family had moved to the house in Hermann Goering Street, only a short distance away from the Chancellery and Hitler, convinced me that the last Nazi *putsch* was about to be enacted. I knew that the original plan of retreating to the Redoubt in Berchtesgaden had been changed some three weeks earlier, although I did not know the reason for the change. Later I had heard the subject of suicide mentioned among the family circle several times. Often I had heard Frau Goebbels say, "Hitler will not die without Goebbels; Goebbels will not die without Hitler; I will not die without Goebbels; Goebbels will not die without the children." In other words, I knew what the plans were: when one died the whole family and the Führer would die. The method of suicide had also been mentioned several times: gas and poison had both been discussed, and I remember Frau Behrend saying, "The only way to give it to the children is to put the poison in a chocolate drink and serve it to them at dinner." It is my belief, therefore, that the poison was administered in this way to the whole group.

When I left the Schwänenburg to drive back to the house in Hermann Goering Street, the Russians were already shelling the area around the Brandenburger Tor. The streets were littered with dead and I had difficulty returning to the house.

Saturday night, 21 April 1945, Goebbels left the house to confer with Hitler in the Chancellery, close by. He returned about 2:30 Sunday morning. He spoke to no one, he looked at no one, and he gave the impression of a broken, finished man. He went upstairs, got a blanket, and went out to join his family in the bunker. A Russian air attack was still in progress.

Sunday noon, 22 April 1945, the Waffen SS men in the house were reinforced, and that afternoon a company of Volkssturm occupied the entire house. The halls inside were barricaded, firing holes had been made in the walls of the house, and the roof was already occupied by snipers.

About four o'clock that afternoon I met Goebbels' personal valet downstairs. I asked him if Goebbels had eaten yet. He replied that he had, but that the majority of the meal, from the soup to the roast duck, was strewn over the table where Goebbels, shaking badly from fright, had spilled it.

Later that afternoon, a kitchen maid asked me for some flour and some sugar to take to her home in North Berlin, which was already threatened by the Russians. I went outside to the storehouse to get it for her. On the way I met Frau Goebbels coming out of the bunker. She was walking unsteadily, feeling her way along the walls. When she saw me, she ran over to me and clasped my arm in both her hands. "My dear Herr Rohrssen," she cried, and continued her unsteady walk toward the house. When I came back from the storehouse, I saw her

201

again, this time returning from the house. She was even more in a daze than earlier; she seemed to see no one. She appeared to be somewhat out of her mind; although she often drank, she was not drunk at the time.

From one of the servants of the Goebbels' children I learned later what happened when she returned to the bunker. As she entered, the children ran up to her. Helmut, her nine-year old son, said, "Mother, you look so happy, you must surely bring us something good. We must be going to meet the Führer!" "Yes, children," she replied, "get ready. You are going to meet the Führer." "Should we take our luggage along?" they asked. "No," she answered. "You won't need your luggage any more." Shortly thereafter they all came out of the bunker.

I was standing nearby when they came out. Frau Goebbels came over to me and put her arms around my neck. "Thank you for everything," she said. "In a half-hour everything will be over." Then she went upstairs with the children to Goebbels.

In a few minutes someone came down and asked for the key to the door through the wall leading to the Chancellery. I couldn't find the key, and the Goebbels family had to go by car to the Chancellery. That was the last I saw of any of them.

The last words that I remember Goebbels speak were in a discussion which he had with some of his intimates in the bunker a day or so before the last *putsch*. I remember him shouting: "The German people is not worthy of victory! They will have to eat less bread, drink less water, and sacrifice more blood before they can expect a victory!"

Later that Sunday afternoon the order came for the Vokssturm to withdraw from the house – it was not to be defended. At the same time, Goebbels' Adjutant, SS *Hauptsturmführer* Schwegermann, told me to take a car and leave Berlin with as many of the personnel of the house as I could take with me. "Thanks for everything," he said. "It's all over now."

I left to go to my apartment and pack my things. On my way I was stopped by *Oberregierungsrat* Fluger, who told me, "You are supposed to come immediately to the Chancellery with all of the personnel of the house. Orders of the Führer." I told him I had already received orders to leave Berlin, wherewith he became excited and repeated his orders. I told him once more that I was leaving and continued to my apartment. There I packed my things in my knapsack. As I finished my door was broken open with an ax and Fluger came into the room. He was now very excited and once more told me it was the Führer's orders that I come to the Chancellery. I told him I would come immediately, and he left the room. I then took my pack and overcoat, jumped out of the window, ran to the car, and drove away with four women of the house personnel and Goebbel's personal valet. We traveled together as far as Burg, near the Elbe, where I left the car and tried to get across the river. For several days I attempted to cross, but there were SS troops everywhere. One day I was called to the District Commander's office and questioned. He stated he had orders to send me back to Berlin. I told him I was there on special business of Dr. Goebbels and showed him a pass I had had for some time. He seemed doubtful and told me to report back the next afternoon. The next day I succeeded in getting across the river.

From there I made my way slowly, partly by foot, partly with a bicycle, until I finally reached my home in Bueckeburg, where my wife was waiting for me.

Where is Hitler's Body?

I know that the last *putsch* was supposed to include Hitler as well as the whole Goebbels family and other intimate members of Hitler's circle. I also know that when I and the rest of the personnel of the house in Hermann Goering Strasse were called to the Chancellery, it was intended that we should be included in the *putsch*. Since we were all told to come to the Chancellery, and since that is where Goebbels and his family went, I assume the poisoning took place in the garden of the Chancellery. It

Jim Hargrove

would be my first assumption, therefore, that because of the haste of the affair and the proximity of the Russians, Hitler was buried in the garden of the Chancellery.

Should this be proved false, however, a second assumption, born of my intimate knowledge of the mentality, logic and flair for showmanship which these men possessed, presents itself to me. Frederic the Great has always been the symbol and shrine of Prussian and Germanic militarism and might. Under the Nazi regime this idealization was continued and prospered. In November 1943, the coffin of Frederic the Great was removed from its tomb in the Garrison's Kirche in Potsdam and moved to a more secure site. Where it was taken, I do not know. It is my belief, however, that should the body of Hitler not be found in the Chancellery garden, it will, to perpetuate the legend of Hitler and to link his name with the first great German hero, be found in or with the coffin of Frederic the Great.

CONFIDENTIAL
CI Targets
Obtained from Wilhelm Rohrssen

BUTLER OF DR. GOEBBELS

EMIL NEUZLAR, 21 Rosenanger, Prchnau (near Berlin), personal butler of Dr. Goebbels. Escaped with Rohrssen, tried to cross the Elbe near Magdeburg, then decided to try to make his way to his family at above address. Supposedly not a party member, and thought to have considerable knowledge of matters concerning the personality of Goebbels and the *Reichspropaganda* Ministry.

BROTHER-IN-LAW OF DR. GOEBBELS

KIMMICH (first name unknown), reported to have fled to southern Germany with his wife (sister of Dr. Goebbels), daughter (age 6 months) and his mother-in-law. Kimmich was film producer and closely liked to propaganda ministry although reported not to have been on the best of terms with Goebbels.

PROPAGANDA MINISTRY

Regierungsrat OTTE, one of the closest co-workers of Dr. Goebbels. Native of Lippe-Detmold, also maintains address in a suburb of Berlin.

Staatssekretär Naumann, chief propaganda brain of Dr. Goebbels, native of Breslau, last residence Berlin-Babelsberg.

Mrs. SEILER, right hand of Dr. Goebbels, fled to Northern Germany in the vicinity of Lübeck. Has daughter, 3-4 years, in Switzerland.

Ministerialrat HAMEL, secretary of Goebbels. Hamel's father has banking house in Berlin (firm has a corporate name other than his own). Hamel and his father were intimate friends of Walter Funk, minister of economics.

PROPAGANDA MINISTRY, DEPARTMENT OF ARTS AND TREASURES

Dr. BIEBERACH, director of office, resident of Berlin.

Mrs. Dr. KOSKA, assistant director of office, resident of Berlin, lives with parents.

Dr. LOHSE, residing in Berlin Steglitz. Art historian, purchasing agent of arts and treasures for Hermann Goering.

Mr. HABERSTOCK, resides in a castle near Bamberg, thoroughly familiar with art purchases made in France.

Dr. BARTELS, born in Braunschweig, reported to have fled to Harz Mountains, vicinity Bad Harzberg. Member of the Kulturkammer (ministry of culture), thoroughly familiar with disposition of national wealth and property.

Architect SCHWEITZER, native of Bremen, last reported residing with parents in Berlin-Dahlem. Thoroughly familiar with purchases (?) of arts and treasures in Holland and France.

CACHES OF ARTS AND TREASURES.

A part of arts treasures have been stowed away in a bunker in Horst Wessel Platz in Berlin. Dr. Schweitzer and Dr. Koska have detailed information.

Another cache is in the bunker at 20 Hermann Goering Strasse. The latter contains among other items safes where microfilms of secret documents were kept. Regierungsrat OTTE has key to these safes. Flat silver of propaganda ministry in special "silver safe" also at 20 Hermann Goering Strasse.

It is reported that, by order of the Mayor of Berlin, Mr. Winkler, who was closely linked with the propaganda ministry, films have been hidden in Castle Bueckeburg and in Bad Oyenhausen.

SICHERHEITSDIENST (SD)

Twenty-two men of the SD were permanently on duty in the house at 20 Hermann Goering Strasse. Some of these personalities were:

Hauptstürmführer ECKHOLT, native of Creiz-Reuss (thought to be head of SD in the House.)
Stürmführer GUNZEL
Stürmführer GANTUSCH
Stürmführer OSWALD

Jim Hargrove

REPORT OF INTERROGATION OF PRISONER OF WAR

Hq, 35th Inf Div
APO 35, U. S. Army
3 April 1945

PWs: Pvt: 1.

EVALUATION: Very intelligent, very willing and cooperative; reliable.

DATE AND PLACE OF CAPTURE: Deserted 3 April 1945 to American Forces at (634294).

PW's UNIT; 3 Co, 77 Repl Bn (KG HESSE), 253 Repl Regt, 26 Inf Div.

OB INFORMATION:

   Units: PW states Kampfgruppe was committed as independent unit in this area, with no connection that he knows of with higher units. Indications of the 253 Repl Regt, with its subordinate Repl Bns, being also brought into the sector are, however, at hand. PW believes 453 Repl Bn, his former unit, to be in Vic GELSENKIRCHEN 95624); furthermore, PW states parking places for 40 trucks were sought when 77 Repl Bn moved N into this sector from former station, whereas a maximum of 9 or 10 trucks were actually used to transport his Kampfgruppe.
   PW states composition of 253 Repl Regt is as follows:

> 77 Repl Bn
> 78 Repl Bn
> 39 Repl Bn
> 453 Repl Bn (Atchd)
> 454 Arty Repl Bn (Atchd)

Directive was received by 77 Repl Bn 25 March 1945 that the Bn (heretofore called Repl and Tng Bn) should be divided into two units – a Repl Bn (now called Gren Ers Bn), and a Tng Bn (called Ausbildung Bn). The Repl Bn was to be composed of men most fit for combat service and to be sent to rear areas of the front for use as reserves or front line troops when necessary. Tng Bns were to be sent to areas further back for Tng and labor work. 77 Tng Bn was accordingly sent to the Vic BIELEFELD when 77 Repl Bn was sent to this sector for commitment. PW states 77 Tng Bn had one Plat which was 4-F: men suffering from dust lung diseases, people with only one leg or one eye, etc. PW further stated it was his impression that the directive was general for all Repl and Tng Bns – that all such Bns should be divided up into groups for front line service and training groups.

Strength: 2 Co, 77 Repl Bn: 80 men
1 Co, 77 Repl Bn: Same
3 Co, 77 Repl Bn: Same

Weapons: 2 Co, 77 Repl Bn – 9 LMGS, 8-10 Pz Fsts, 3-4 MP *44s, 7-8 "Schnellfeuer Gewehre" (M-1s), 4-5 Handgrenaden, 1 Rifle Grenade Launcher w/15 rds Rifle Grenades, but no cartridges for their discharge, 98K rifles

1 Co, 77 Repl Bn – PW thinks similarly equipped.

3 Co, 77 Repl Bn – Same

Personalities: CO, 77 Repl Bn (KG HESSE): Hptm HESSE
CO, 2 Co, 77 Repl Bn: Lt. Spricker
CO, 3 Co, 77 Repl Bn: Lt Kalduhn
CO, 253 Repl Bn (PW states he is no longer Regtl CO, but also states he was seen in this Vic 1 April): Obst FEIND
CO, 453 Repl Bn; Formerly Maj ECHTERMAN, replaced by Hptm CREMER; PW believes he too has been replaced

Locations:
Units: 77 Tng Bn: Vic BIELEFELD
39 Repl & Tng Bn: Vic AFFELN in SAUERLAND 27 March
454 Repl & Tng Bn: Vic Plattenburg in SAUERLAND 27 March
2 Co, 77 Repl Bn:
1 Plat: In Posn Vic (634288), E of HERNE (6427)
2 Plat: In Posn Vic (638289), W of HERNE
1 Co, 77 Repl Bn: Right of 2 Co
3 Co, 77 Repl Bn: Right of 2 Co
CPs: 2 Co, 77 Repl Bn: In House at (636289) night of 2 April
77 Repl Bn: In House at (636283) 2 April
MLR: Runs parallel to RHINE-HERNE Canal 200-300 yds S of Canal

BRIDGES AND CROSSING SITES:
Bridge over EMSCHER Canal on HERNE-RECKLINGHAUSEN Rd (foot)

Bridge over RHINE-HERNE Canal on HERNE-RECK'HAUSEN Rd still passable by foot although 4-5 yards are under water.

Ferry Vic (625237) still transporting civilians noon 2 April

PW believes ventilating shaft exists leading from RECKLINGHAUSEN ZECHE (628294) under canals to other side.

AT Obstacles: Obstacles (iron stakes set loosely in ground) before Bridges over

RHINE-HERNE and EMSCHER Canals on HERNE-RECKLINGHAUSEN Road.

Obstacle of same type at (638288).

Miscellaneous: Kitchen 2 Co, 77 Repl Bn: Vic (638288)

ARTILLERY:

Locations: 3 20-mm Quadruple Mt AA Guns Vic (639289)
4 (?) 88-mm Pak-Flak Guns Vic (635276)

Supply and Ammunition:

PW states English air bomb duds are being used for demolition work.

MORALE: Troops on other side of Canal poorly equipped, poorly trained, have no desire to fight on. Only fear of getting shot and the propaganda about the bad treatment they will receive as prisoners keeps them from deserting. Civilians resent soldiers sheltering themselves in or near their houses; Volkssturm is called up, but is used mostly as labor battalion; they are poorly armed and have almost no training. PW believes they will throw away weapons and uniforms if Americans approach.

MISCELLANEOUS: PW was told they were the last defense line before GELSENKIRCHEN, and they must therefore hold the Posn at all costs. PW says civilians were supposed to be evacuated from HERNE morning 3 April, but does not think they will leave.

GEORGE D. BUXBAUM
1ST LT, QMC
OIC, IPW Team 138

Jim Hargrove

ARREST REPORT

Surname: SONNTAG   First Name(s) HEINRICH
        Alias: NONE

Nationality claimed: German

Address of Last Residence: B R A K E, Detmolderstrasse 60

Occupation: Farmer and innkeeper

Identity Documents: Ausmusterungschein
                    (Deferment Certificate)

Details of Arrest: (a) Place: L E M G O
                       (b) Date: 7 May 1945
                       (c) Time: 1500

Unit Making Arrest: XVI Corps   CIC Det.

Reason for Arrest: Ortsgruppenleiter in Brake 1933-34, member of Party since 1931, active Nazi up until moment troops took town.   Accused of subversive activities after occupation (see attached statements). Deemed a security threat, and recommend that he be interned.

Statement After Arrest: Admits Party membership since 1931, admits being Ortsgruppenleiter 1933-34. Denies any subversive activities.

Property: (Property taken from prisoner to be listed on back)
            With the body.

Jim Hargrove

Military or Civil Authority Taking Custody of the Prisoner:
Provost Marshall, 666 FA Bn.

Signature of person authorizing arrest:
                       J. W. Hargrove   Rank: M Sgt
                       XVI Corps CIC

Date: 8 May 1945

ABOUT THE AUTHOR

Jim Hargrove, Senior

Jim Hargrove was born in Shreveport, Louisiana but has lived most of his life in Houston, Texas. He graduated from Sewanee Military Academy and Rice University, where he majored in philosophy, studied languages, and was elected to Phi Beta Kappa. He enlisted in the army and served in the European Theater of Operations in IPW Team 138; he was discharged in January 1946 as a Master Sergeant. After the War he became a corporate executive, served as Senior Assistant Postmaster General of the United States, and was appointed U. S. Ambassador to Australia in 1976. After his return, he joined an investment management firm in Houston and served on corporate and non-profit boards. He is married, with four children and seven grandchildren.

The Way It Was is his first publication.